Usborne Spotter's Guides Night Sky

Sam Smith

Designed by Karen Tomlins

Astronomy consultants:
Stuart Atkinson and Steve Hateley

With thanks to stellarium.org for use of their star maps

You can use this book to help you spot all sorts of things in the Northern Hemisphere's night sky.

How to use this book

This guide will help you spot moons, planets, stars, and lots of other sights that you can see when you look up at the night sky.

Stargazers use patterns of stars called **CONSTELLATIONS** to map out the sky. Try to imagine lines between their stars to spot these patterns more easily. Here are some of the ones you can look for and explore...

This is Leo the lion, who prowls through spring skies.

Pegasus the winged horse gallops up into the sky in the fall.

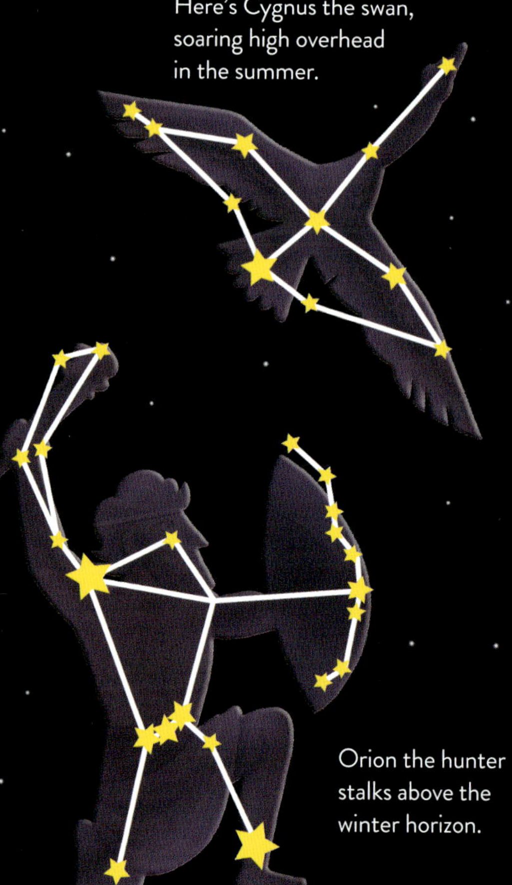

Here's Cygnus the swan, soaring high overhead in the summer.

Orion the hunter stalks above the winter horizon.

Seasonal stars

You'll see different stars in the sky at different times of year. Many of the things to spot in this book are organized into the seasons when it's best to see them.

When and how to spot things

You need the right conditions for stargazing, especially for things that are trickier to spot...

Clear skies

Check the weather forecast before you head out – you won't be able to see much if it's too cloudy.

Dark, open places

Town or city lights can make the stars difficult to see. This is called **light pollution**. Try to go to a dark, open place where your view isn't blocked by any tall buildings or trees.

Your eyes need 20 to 30 minutes to fully adjust to the dark, so try not to use phones or flashlights once you're ready.

Always take a grown-up with you when you go out to look at the night sky.

The Moon

The best time to spot things is when the Moon is dark. When it's too full and bright, its light can outshine lots of other sights.

Stargazing isn't easy, and it takes lots of practice and patience. You won't always find what you're looking for, but don't give up – it's worth it when you do!

Seeing further

You can see lots of constellations just by looking up at the night sky. But with binoculars or a telescope, you can "zoom in" to see even more sights inside them.

What can you see?

The red circles in this book show what you might see when you look at each sight through a telescope.

Telescope view of the Pleiades (p. 55)

How to see it?

Fact boxes tell you the scientific names that are used to label sights inside constellations. They also tell you how to look for things, and how hard they are to spot, from ✶ (easy) to ✶ ✶ ✶ ✶ ✶ (very tricky).

Scientific name: Messier 45 (M45)
Visibility: even in light-polluted skies
Look with: naked eye or binoculars
Difficulty to spot: ✶

Binoculars

You can see some wonderful views of the Moon and star clusters when exploring the night sky with binoculars.

A good binocular size to use is 10 x 50. This means that they magnify things ten times, and that each front lens is 50mm (2in) wide.

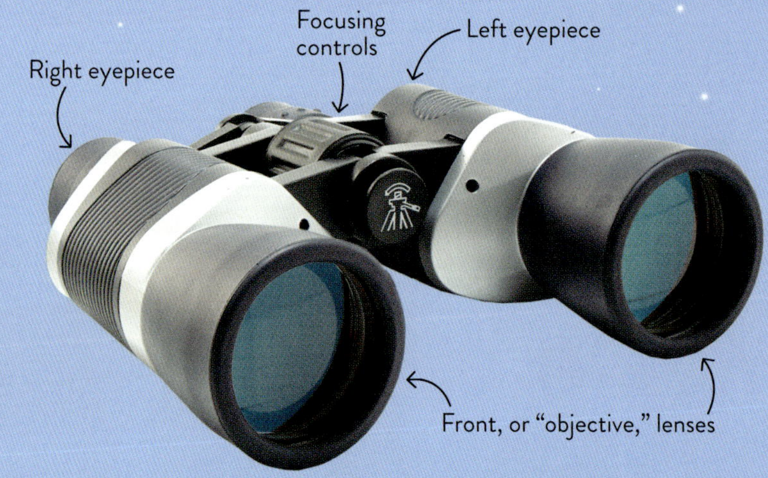

Bigger binoculars can show you more, but they're heavy and hard to hold steady, so it's best to mount them on a tripod.

Telescopes

Telescopes show you a lot more than binoculars. The size of their main mirror or lens is what affects how much more you'll see with one.

You can use different eyepieces to change the magnification of a telescope.

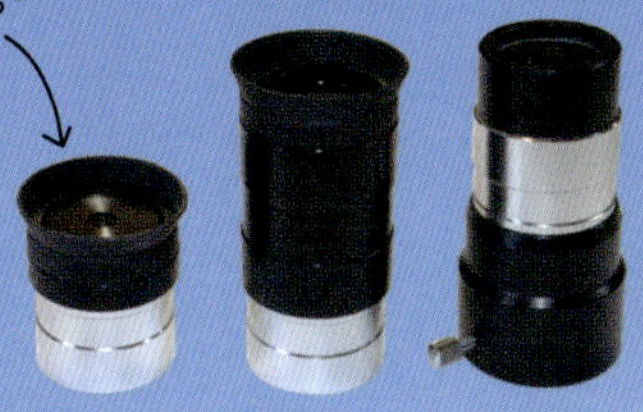

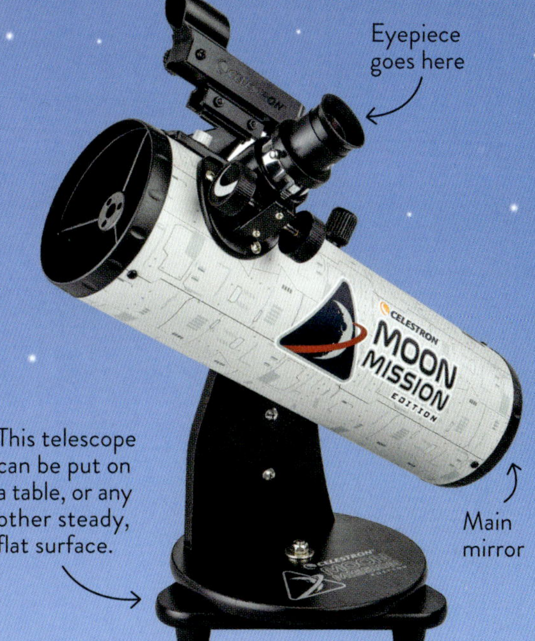

Eyepiece goes here
CELESTRON
MOON MISSION
EDITION
This telescope can be put on a table, or any other steady, flat surface.
Main mirror

Pointing your telescope

Many telescopes have a red dot finder (RDF) to help aim them. To use one, keep both eyes open a little way behind the RDF, then slowly move the telescope until the dot is where you want to look.

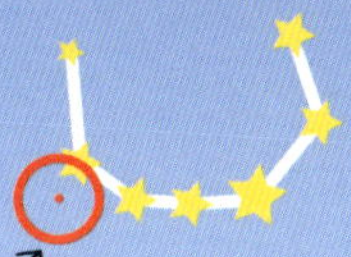
The red circles on diagrams show where to aim your RDF.

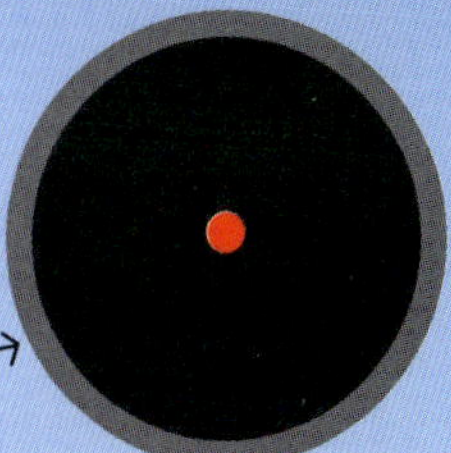
You can reduce the red dot's brightness to see fainter stars to help you aim.

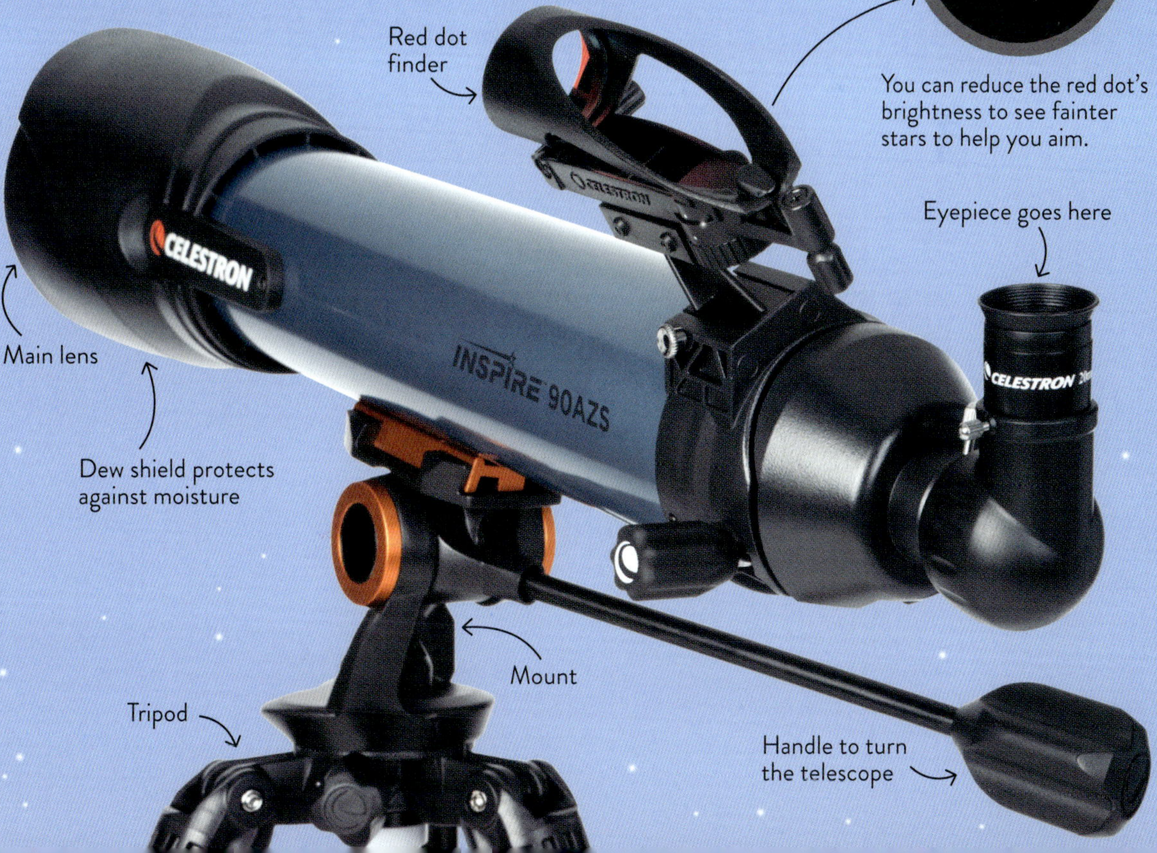
Red dot finder
Eyepiece goes here
CELESTRON
INSPIRE 90AZS
Main lens
Dew shield protects against moisture
Mount
Tripod
Handle to turn the telescope

What is there to see?

Here are some of the amazing things you can spot in the night sky.

Planets

The other planets that orbit the Sun reflect its light, so they look like stars in our night sky – until you take a closer look!

Jupiter

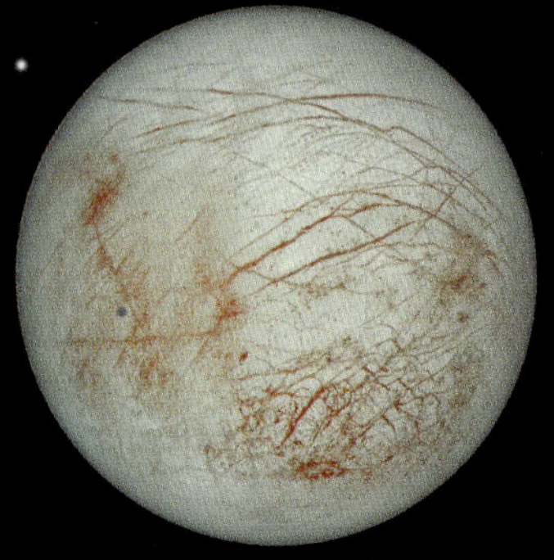

Europa is one of Jupiter's moons.

Moons

There are lots of things to spot on our own Moon (p. 10–13), and you can make out some of the moons that orbit other planets in the Solar System, too.

Double stars

A double star is two stars that are very close together in the sky. Some are pairs of stars that orbit around each other, but others only *appear* close together because they are lined up from our point of view.

Variable stars

These stars shine brighter or dimmer as they swell and shrink, or when another star that orbits them blocks out some of their light.

Open clusters

These are groups of bright, young stars that were all born from the same giant gas cloud. The stars slowly drift apart over hundreds of millions of years.

Open clusters are made up of a few hundred to a few thousand stars.

Globular clusters

Much bigger, older and more tightly-packed than open clusters, these giant star-globes can contain hundreds of thousands of stars, and exist for billions of years.

Nebulas

Some of these clouds of dust and gas are huge regions where new stars are born. Others are smaller (but still very large), and are created when a dying star sheds its outer gases.

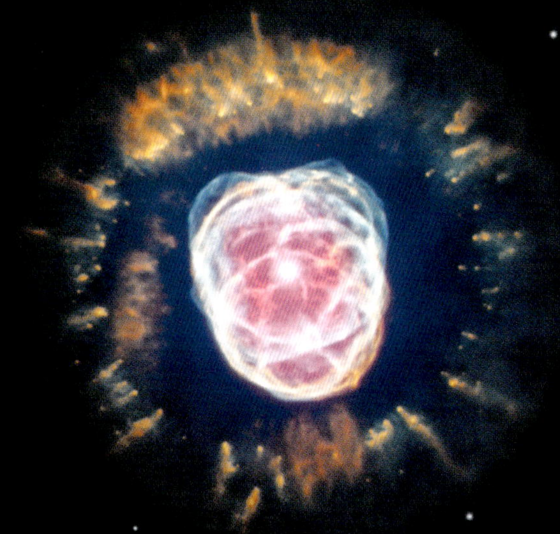

Galaxies

These vast collections of billions or trillions of stars can be various shapes, including spirals and ovals. They're the only sights you'll see that aren't in our own galaxy – the Milky Way.

"Different" Moons

Although our Moon is always the same, the way it looks in our sky changes as the Sun's light moves across it.

The Moon goes through these eight phases every 29.5 days. As it grows fuller, it's said to be "waxing." As it becomes less full, it's "waning."

New Moon

When none of the Moon's near side is lit up, the night sky is much darker and perfect for stargazing.

Crescent Moon

When only a sliver of the Moon is showing, it's still a good time to stargaze, and to look for things on that part of the Moon, too.

Quarter Moon

When around half of the Moon is lit up, try looking close to the line between light and shadow to see some of its best sights.

Gibbous Moon

When more than half of the Moon is showing, its brightness makes stargazing tricky. But you can still try to spot lots of things on the Moon itself.

Full Moon

Enjoy the magical sight of the Moon's entire near side lit up. Its light outshines all other sights in the sky, making them much harder to spot.

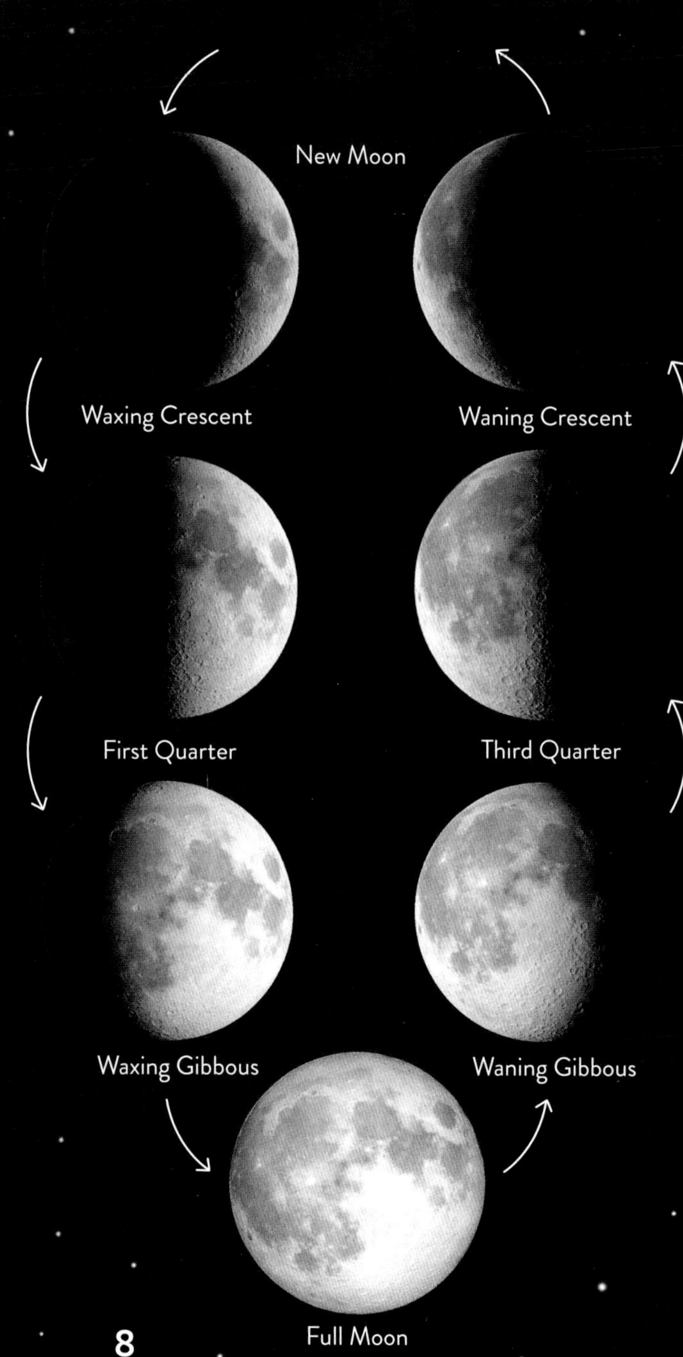

Super Moon

The Moon is sometimes closer to the Earth, and sometimes further away. When there's a Full Moon while it's closest to us, it looks magnificently big and bright.

You can see a Super Moon about three or four times a year.

Speeding Space Station

If you look at the right time, you can occasionally see a small, shadowy shape sweep across the Moon's face in less than a second. That's the International Space Station (p. 60) moving in front of it, as it zips around the Earth with people on board!

Blood Moon

This is a spookier name for a "total lunar eclipse." This happens when the Sun, Earth and Moon line up so that the Earth blocks the Sun's light, casting the Moon in shadow. Some red light still gets through the Earth's atmosphere, which turns the Moon the color of blood.

There are at least two total lunar eclipses every three years.

We always see the same side of the Moon facing us. It's called the "near side." Take a look at what you can see on the Moon's near side on pages 10–13.

Looking at the Moon

Here are some of the things on the Moon that you can try to spot.

The Moon's dark **"seas"** are actually huge plains of frozen lava from ancient, extinct volcanoes.

Rilles are long, narrow grooves that look like dried-up riverbeds.

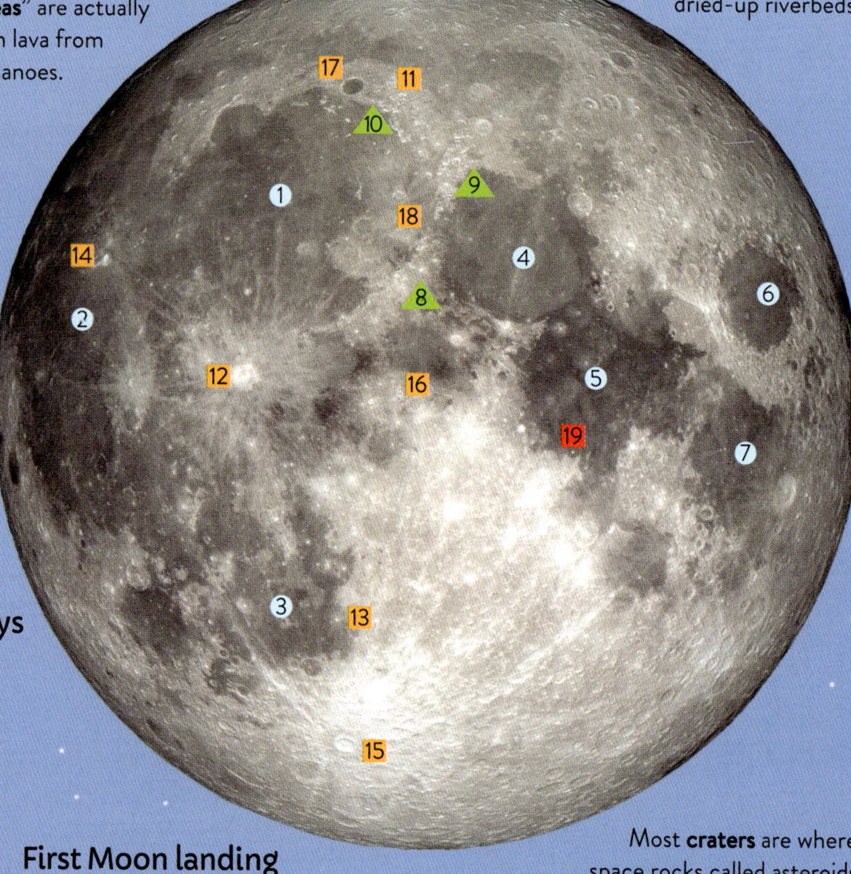

Major seas

1 Sea of Rains
2 Ocean of Storms
3 Sea of Clouds
4 Sea of Serenity
5 Sea of Tranquility
6 Sea of Crises
7 Sea of Fertility

Mountain ranges

8 Montes Apenninus
9 Montes Caucasus
10 Montes Alpes

Craters, rilles & valleys

11 Vallis Alpes
12 Copernicus Crater
13 Rupes Recta
14 Aristarchus Crater
15 Tycho Crater
16 Rima Hyginus
17 Plato Crater
18 Hadley Rille

First Moon landing

19 Tranquility Base

Most **craters** are where space rocks called asteroids crashed into the Moon long ago.

8 Montes Apenninus

These are the tallest mountains on the Moon. When they're lit from the side, you can see the huge, looming shadows they cast over the Moon's surface.

When: look for their long shadows at the First Quarter *(see page 8)*
Look with: telescope
Difficulty to spot: ✶ ✶

11 Vallis Alpes

This huge valley runs for 166km (103 miles) through the Montes Alpes. A narrow rille runs down its middle, carved out by lava that once flooded the valley from the "seas" at either end.

When: just after the First Quarter, or just before the Third Quarter *(see page 8)*
Look with: telescope
Difficulty to spot: ✶ ✶ ✶

The rille is *very* hard to see. Can you make out its thin line at the center of the valley in this photo?

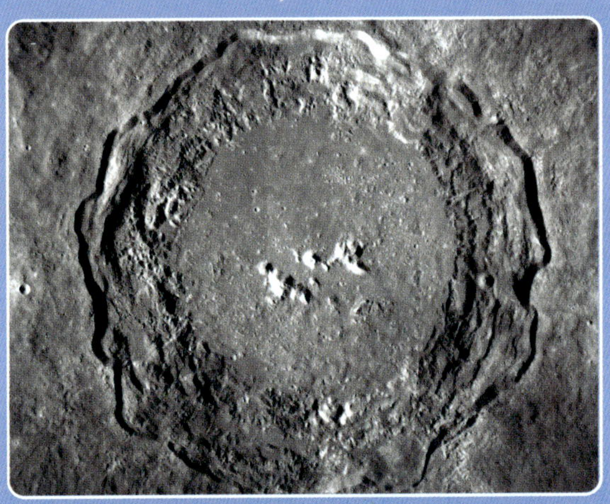

12 Copernicus Crater

The bright spot in the Moon's seas. The splotch around it is debris that was blasted out by the asteroid's impact. Look closer to see the stepped slope of the crater's rim, like Rome's Colosseum.

When: just after the First Quarter, or at the Third Quarter *(see page 8)*
Look with: binoculars or telescope
Difficulty to spot: ✶ ✶

13 Rupes Recta

Also called the "Straight Wall," this steep slope is as tall as the Eiffel Tower. It casts a hair-like shadow at the First Quarter. Two weeks later, it glints like a sword on the waning Moon's face.

When: just after the First Quarter, or at the Third Quarter *(see page 8)*
Look with: telescope
Difficulty to spot: ✶ ✶ ✶ ✶

More on the Moon

14 Aristarchus Crater

This crater is deeper than the Grand Canyon in Arizona, and it's the brightest crater on the Moon. Nearby is the Herodotus Crater and a snaking channel called Schröter's Valley.

When: a few days before or after the Full Moon *(see page 8)*
Look with: telescope
Difficulty to spot: ✶ ✶ ✶

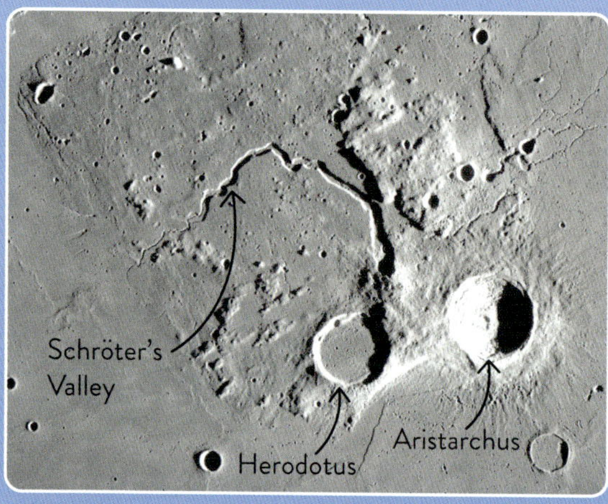

15 Tycho Crater

Can you spot the peak in the middle of this crater? The bright area around Tycho is rock that was blasted out by the asteroid that made it, and is larger than California!

When: a few days before or after the Full Moon *(see page 8)*
Look with: naked eye or telescope
Difficulty to spot: ✶ ✶

16 Rima Hyginus

This long channel branches out from the small crater of an old volcano, and was probably carved out by lava long ago. You might spot smaller craters along its length, too.

When: just after the First Quarter or just before the Third Quarter *(see page 8)*
Look with: telescope
Difficulty to spot: ✶ ✶ ✶ ✶

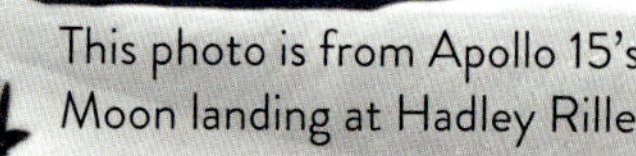

This photo is from Apollo 15's Moon landing at Hadley Rille.

17 Plato Crater

Almost perfectly round, this 3.8-billion-year-old crater was called the "Greater Black Lake" on early Moon maps. Full of frozen, ancient lava, its floor is one of the darkest patches on the Moon.

When: just after the First Quarter and just before the Third Quarter *(see page 8)*
Look with: binoculars or telescope
Difficulty to spot: ✶ ✶ ✶

18 Hadley Rille

Boulders the size of houses are littered over this long, winding canyon's floor. In 1971, Apollo 15's astronauts drove their Moon Rover right up to its edge to take photos.

When: at the First Quarter or a few days after the Full Moon *(see page 8)*
Look with: telescope
Difficulty to spot: ✶ ✶ ✶ ✶ ✶

19 First Moon Landing

In 1969, NASA's Apollo 11 mission landed humans on the Moon for the first time. Neil Armstrong and Buzz Aldrin stepped out onto its dusty surface in the Sea of Tranquility.

When: four or five days after the New Moon or the Full Moon *(see page 8)*
Look with: naked eye or binoculars
Difficulty to spot: ✶ ✶

Planets

Seven other planets orbit our Sun, and you can see them all in the night sky.

The planets' positions change each night, but there are lots of apps and websites that can show you where to look.

Mercury

The smallest planet is tricky to spot because it's so close to the Sun. Try to find it just before sunrise and just after sunset, glinting like a star close to the horizon.

Scientific name: Mercury
Visibility: even in light-polluted skies
Look with: naked eye or binoculars
Difficulty to spot: ✶ ✶ ✶

Be very careful not to look directly at the Sun when you're trying to spot Mercury!

Venus

Boiling-hot Venus is called the "Morning Star" and the "Evening Star" because it gleams brightly before sunrise and after sunset. The Moon is the only thing that's brighter in our night sky.

With a telescope, you can see that Venus waxes and wanes like the Moon.

Scientific name: Venus
Visibility: even in light-polluted skies
Look with: naked eye or telescope
Difficulty to spot: ✶

Mars

Dusty, rust-colored Mars looks like an orange star. When it's closest to us, you can try to see white ice caps at its top and bottom.

Scientific name: Mars
Visibility: even in light-polluted skies
Look with: naked eye or telescope
Difficulty to spot: ✶

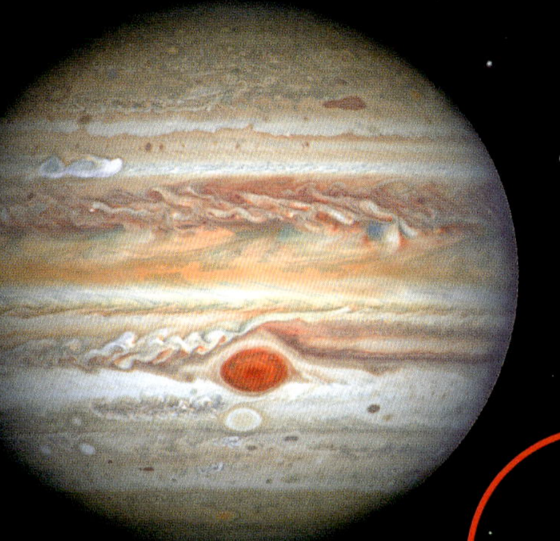

Jupiter

The largest planet in the Solar System outshines all of the stars. See if you can spot its bands of cloud and the famous Great Red Spot – a vast, whirling storm that's been raging for centuries.

Scientific name: Jupiter
Visibility: even in light-polluted skies
Look with: naked eye or telescope
Difficulty to spot: ✶

You might be able to see four of Jupiter's moons as bright dots close to it as well.

Saturn

Zoom in on this ringed planet and you'll see its pretty golden color, and maybe its biggest moon, Titan, as a nearby pinprick of light.

Scientific name: Saturn
Visibility: dark skies
Look with: naked eye or telescope
Difficulty to spot: ✶ ✶

You can only see Saturn's spectacular rings of dust with a powerful telescope.

Uranus

Neptune

Uranus and Neptune

Both of these "ice giant" planets look like pale blue discs when you find them. Neptune is a tough one to spot because it's so far away.

Scientific names: Uranus and Neptune
Visibility: very dark skies
Look with: telescope
Difficulty to spot: ✶ ✶ ✶ ✶

Spring star maps

To use these star maps, face either north or south during the spring. Then, compare the map for that direction to the stars you can see in the sky.

The constellations which are best seen in the spring are shown in green.

LOOKING NORTH

Western horizon

Eastern horizon

LOOKING SOUTH

Eastern horizon

Western horizon

These maps are approximate guides for where to look – your view of the stars changes depending on where you are and the time of night.

Spring star patterns

Can you see a ladle-shaped pattern of bright stars high in the sky? That's the "Big Dipper." You can use it to find lots of other patterns in the spring sky.

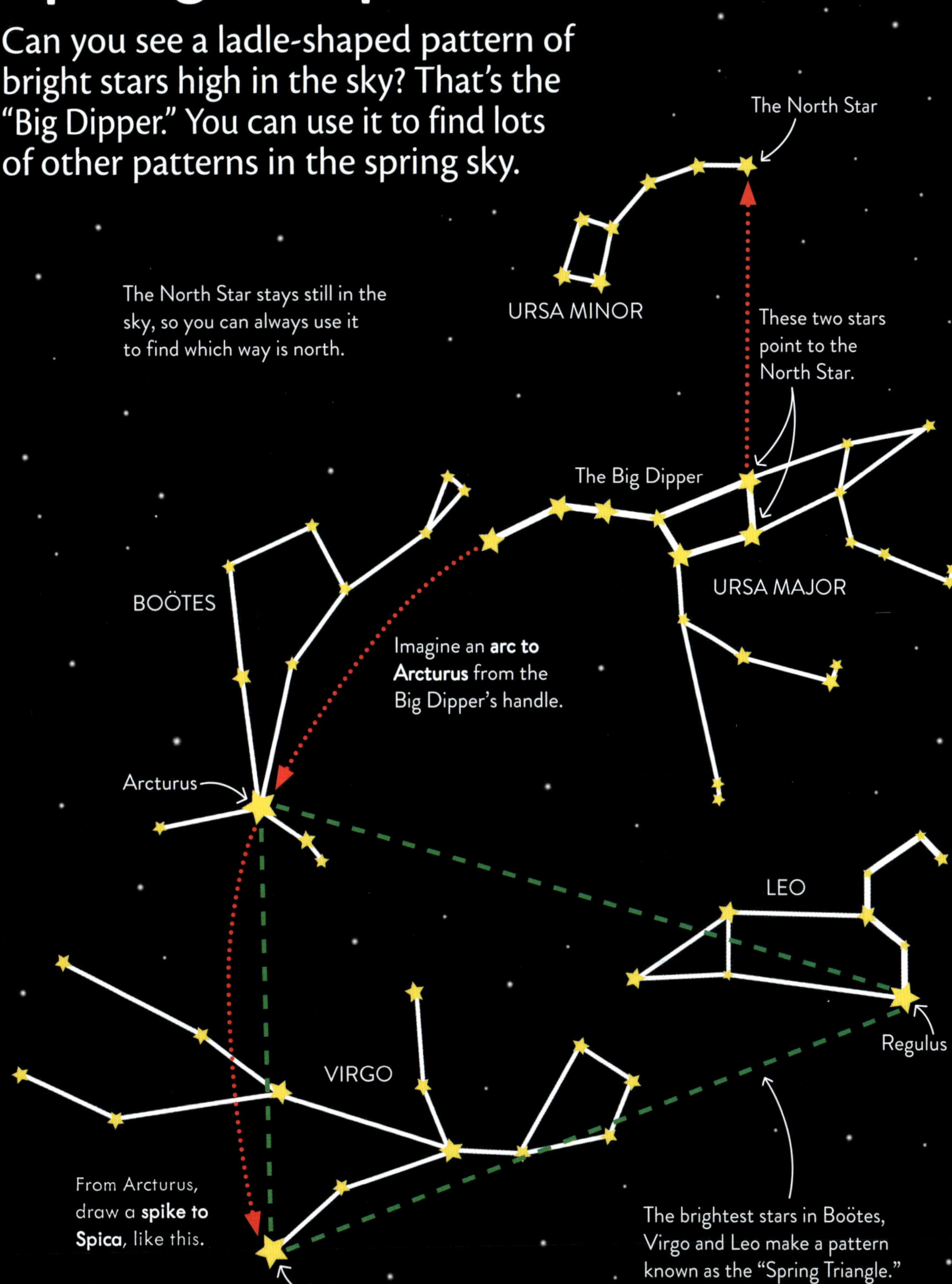

Ursa Major area

Ursa Major means the "Great Bear." In the spring, you can look for lots of galaxies in this part of the sky.

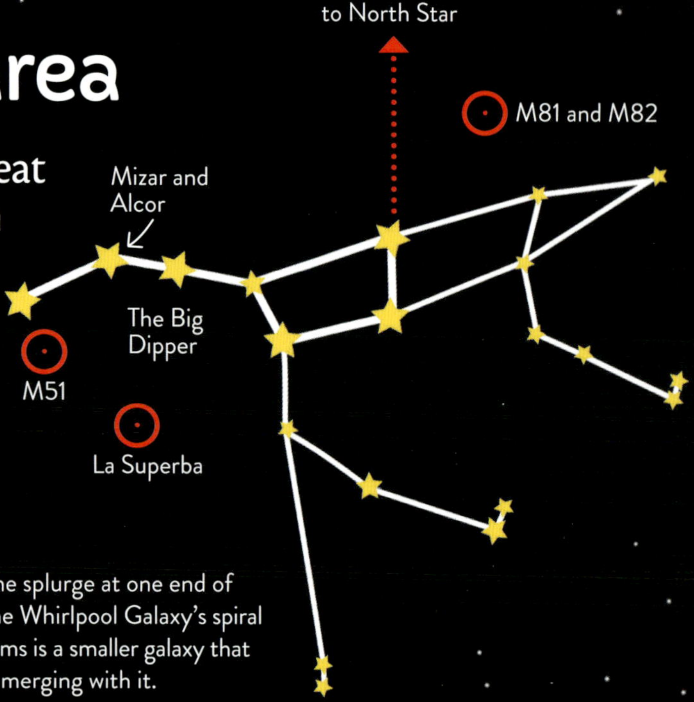

to North Star

M81 and M82

Mizar and Alcor

The Big Dipper

M51

La Superba

The ladle-shaped part of Ursa Major, the Big Dipper, is easy to spot all year round.

The splurge at one end of the Whirlpool Galaxy's spiral arms is a smaller galaxy that is merging with it.

The Whirlpool Galaxy

This beautiful galaxy got its name because it was the first one whose swirling, spiral structure astronomers were able to see.

M51

Scientific name: Messier 51 (M51)
Visibility: very dark skies
Look with: telescope
Difficulty to spot: ✶ ✶ ✶ ✶ ✶

Mizar and Alcor

Nicknamed the "horse and rider," this famous double star was used as an eyesight test in ancient times. If you could see both stars, it was (and still is!) a sign of excellent vision.

Scientific name: Mizar and Alcor
Visibility: even in light-polluted skies
Look with: naked eye or binoculars
Difficulty to spot: ✶

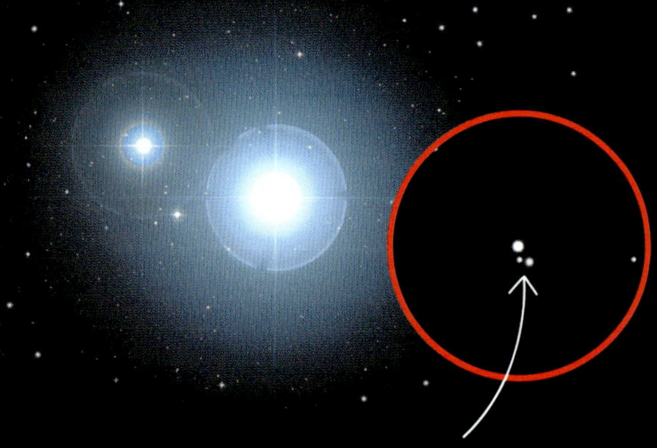

Mizar is actually four stars, and Alcor is two, so in fact you're looking at six stars in all.

La Superba

One of the reddest stars discovered, “La Superba means “the magnificent one” in Italian. It has a “sooty” atmosphere which filters out other colors of light, making it shine like a ruby.

Scientific name: Y Canum Venaticorum
Visibility: even in light-polluted skies
Look with: telescope
Difficulty to spot: ✶ ✶

The Cigar Galaxy

We can only see the edge of this galaxy, so it looks like a thin cigar. At its core, new stars are being born ten times faster than in all parts of the Milky Way combined!

Scientific name: Messier 82 (M82)
Visibility: dark skies
Look with: telescope
Difficulty to spot: ✶ ✶ ✶ ✶

Bode’s Galaxy

You’ll find this bright galaxy right next to the Cigar Galaxy. Its powerful gravity is pulling gas into its smaller neighbor’s core, which is why so many new stars are being born there.

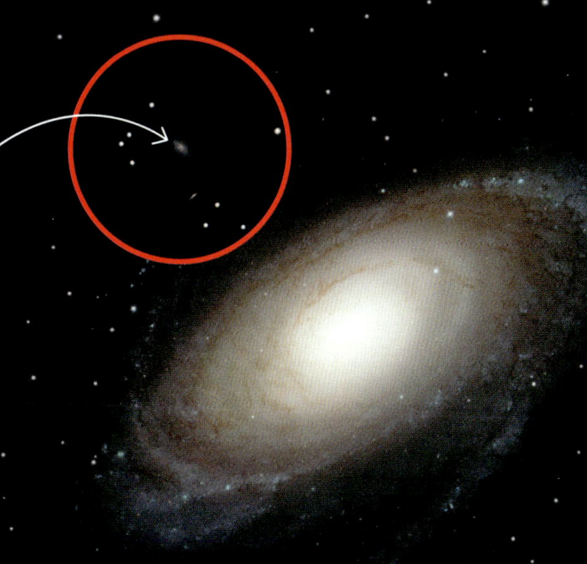

Scientific name: Messier 81 (M81)
Visibility: dark skies
Look with: telescope
Difficulty to spot: ✶ ✶ ✶ ✶

Boötes & nearby

This constellation looks a bit like a giant kite, with the bright, orangey star Arcturus at the bottom.

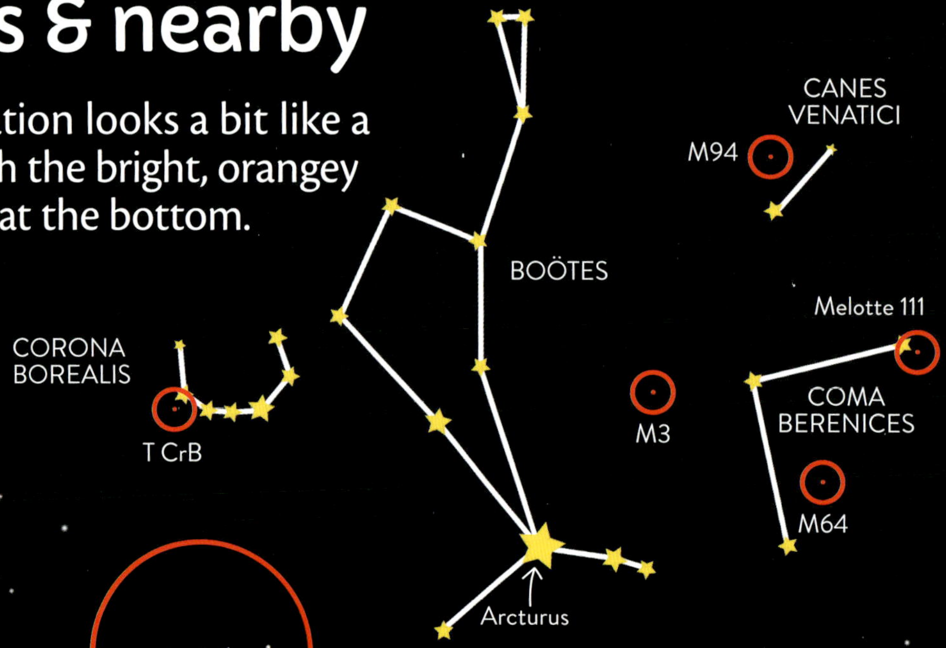

CANES VENATICI
M94
BOÖTES
Melotte 111
CORONA BOREALIS
T CrB
M3
COMA BERENICES
M64
Arcturus

Messier 3 Globular Cluster

One of the biggest and brightest in the sky. Its half a million stars are over 11 billion years old, and at least 274 are variable stars – by far the most found in any globular cluster.

Scientific name: Messier 3 (M3)
Visibility: dark skies
Look with: telescope
Difficulty to spot: ✶ ✶ ✶

The Cat's Eye Galaxy

Astronomers think this galaxy contains about 40 billion stars – less than half as many as our own. The outer "ring" you can see is actually two separate spiral arms.

Scientific name: Messier 94 (M94)
Visibility: dark skies
Look with: telescope
Difficulty to spot: ✶ ✶ ✶ ✶

The Black Eye Galaxy

A dark band of dust blocks out some of the light from this spiral galaxy's bright core. This feature has earned it various names – the "Black Eye Galaxy," the "Evil Eye Galaxy" and the "Sleeping Beauty Galaxy."

Scientific name: Messier 64 (M64)
Visibility: dark skies
Look with: telescope
Difficulty to spot: ✶ ✶ ✶ ✶

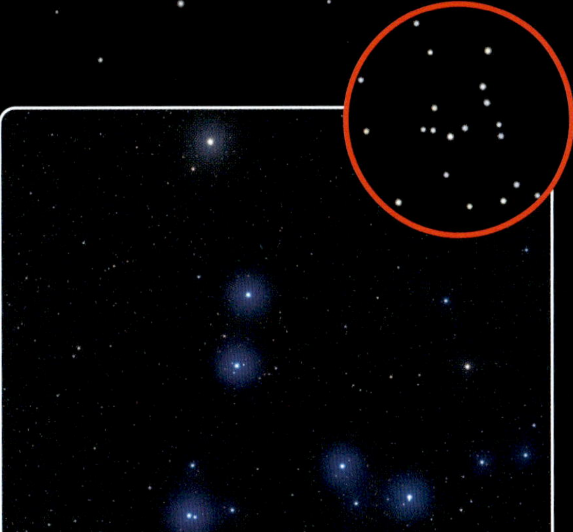

The Coma Star Cluster

Stargazers long ago imagined this cluster as the flowing hair of the Egyptian queen Berenice II ("coma" is "hair" in Latin). Spot the "V" shape of its brightest stars, spread over a wide patch of sky.

Scientific name: Melotte 111
Visibility: even in light-polluted skies
Look with: binoculars or telescope
Difficulty to spot: ✶ ✶

The Blaze Star

About every 80 years, this star blazes brightly for a few days. It's actually two stars – a smaller one stealing gas off a nearby giant. Eventually, that gas gets so hot that there's a bright explosion on the smaller star.

Scientific name: T Coronae Borealis (T CrB)
Visibility: dark skies
Look with: binoculars or telescope
Difficulty to spot: ✶ ✶ ✶

Leo & Cancer

A pattern of stars at the front of Leo (the lion) is shaped like a backwards question mark. It's called the "Sickle."

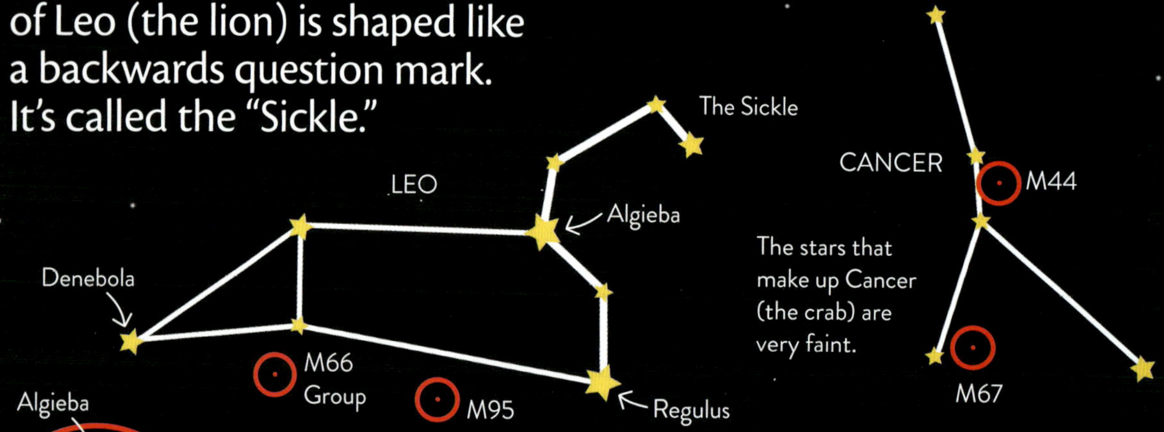

The Sickle

LEO

Algieba

Denebola

M66 Group

M95

Regulus

CANCER

M44

The stars that make up Cancer (the crab) are very faint.

M67

Algieba

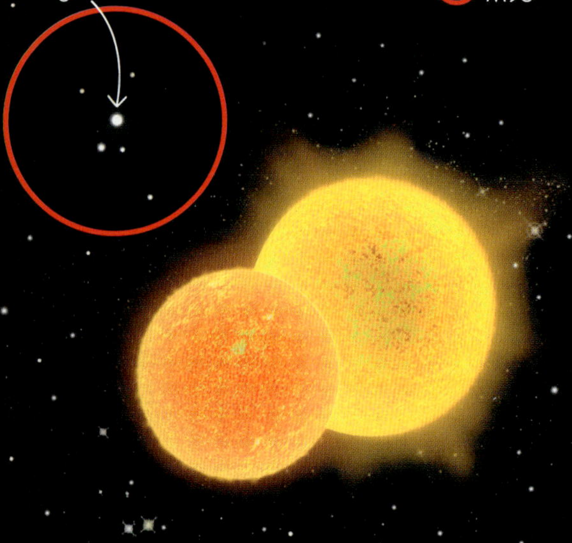

Algieba

The second-brightest star in Leo is actually two stars orbiting each other. The brighter one has at least one planet, which is over eight times more massive than Jupiter!

Scientific name: Gamma Leonis
Visibility: even in light-polluted skies
Look with: naked eye; telescope to split
Difficulty to spot: ★

The King Cobra Cluster

One of the most ancient open clusters. Its stars are around four billion years old (about the age of the Sun), so it's a perfect place for us to search for solar systems like ours.

Scientific name: Messier 67 (M67)
Visibility: dark skies
Look with: telescope
Difficulty to spot: ★ ★ ★ ★

The Leo Triplet

A spectacular group of three spiral galaxies, all fighting a mighty tug-of-war as they pull each other out of shape with their gravity. One of them, which looks thin and flat in our sky, is nicknamed the "Hamburger Galaxy."

Scientific name: Messier 66 (M66) Group
Visibility: very dark skies
Look with: telescope
Difficulty to spot: ✶ ✶ ✶ ✶

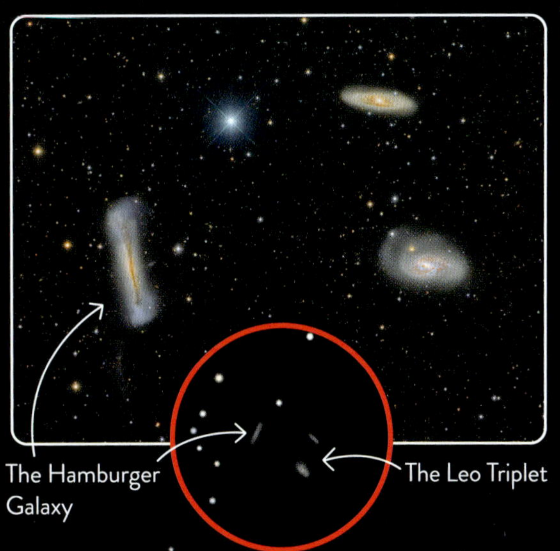

The Beehive Cluster

One of the closest open clusters to us, the Beehive is a small blur to your eyes. But take a look through binoculars, and it will transform into a magical swarm of about 20 stars.

Scientific name: Messier 44 (M44)
Visibility: dark skies
Look with: binoculars or telescope
Difficulty to spot: ✶ ✶ ✶

Messier 95 Spiral Galaxy

This galaxy's spiral arms wind very tightly around its blazing, golden core. They're dotted with lots of sparkling clusters of young, blue stars.

Scientific name: Messier 95 (M95)
Visibility: very dark skies
Look with: telescope
Difficulty to spot: ✶ ✶ ✶ ✶ ✶

Virgo & nearby

This area of sky is full of galaxies. You can use the bright star Spica to find Virgo.

M87
VIRGO
M61
M104
Spica
NGC 4361
CORVUS
M68

The center of a group of up to 2,000 galaxies is in Virgo. It's called the "Virgo Cluster."

The Sombrero Galaxy

A dark lane of dust makes this galaxy's outer disc look like the wide brim of a sombrero (a Mexican sun hat).

Scientific name: Messier 104 (M104)
Visibility: very dark skies
Look with: telescope
Difficulty to spot: ✶ ✶ ✶ ✶ ✶

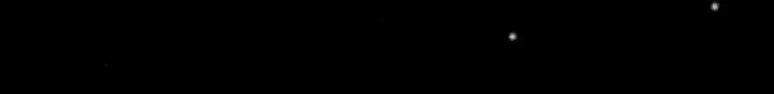

Dust lane

Messier 68 Globular Cluster

The brightest stars in this ancient cluster burned out long ago, so only old, dim ones are left. It can be tricky to spot as it lies very low on the southern horizon.

Scientific name: Messier 68 (M68)
Visibility: dark skies
Look with: telescope
Difficulty to spot: ✶ ✶ ✶ ✶

Virgo A Galaxy

At this huge galaxy's heart is a monster of a black hole that's 6.5 billion times more massive than the Sun! In 2017, the Event Horizon Telescope's images of it (*see top left*) were the first ones ever taken of a black hole.

Scientific name: Messier 87 (M87)
Visibility: dark skies
Look with: telescope
Difficulty to spot: ✶ ✶ ✶ ✶

The Garden Sprinkler Nebula

This nebula's unusual name comes from the "S"-shaped jets of hot gas that are firing out from its central dying star – like spinning jets of water spraying a lawn.

Scientific name: NGC 4361
Visibility: dark skies
Look with: telescope
Difficulty to spot: ✶ ✶ ✶ ✶ ✶

At least six huge star explosions called "supernovas" have been seen inside M61 – among the most in any galaxy.

The Swelling Spiral Galaxy

About the same size as our own, this galaxy is hungrily using up vast amounts of the gases inside it to create lots of new stars very quickly.

Scientific name: Messier 61 (M61)
Visibility: very dark skies
Look with: telescope
Difficulty to spot: ✶ ✶ ✶ ✶ ✶

Summer star maps

To use these star maps, face either north or south during the summer. Then, compare the map for that direction to the stars you can see in the sky.

The constellations which are best seen in the summer are shown in pink.

LOOKING NORTH

Western horizon

Eastern horizon

LOOKING SOUTH

Eastern horizon

Western horizon

These maps are approximate guides for where to look – your view of the stars changes depending on where you are and the time of night.

Summer star patterns

Look east around nightfall. Can you spot a sparkling blue-white star, high in the sky? That's Vega, which you can use to find lots of nearby star patterns.

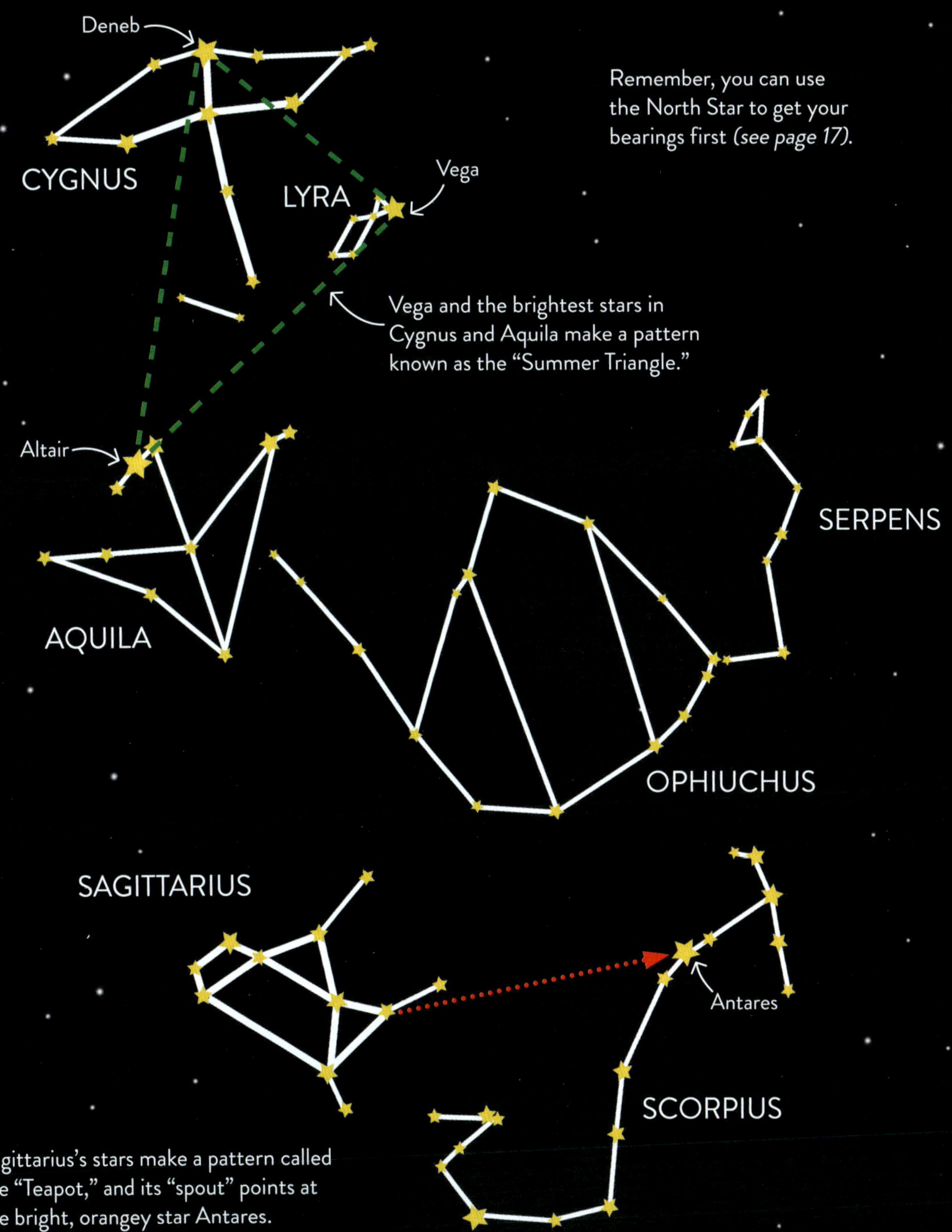

Remember, you can use the North Star to get your bearings first *(see page 17)*.

Vega and the brightest stars in Cygnus and Aquila make a pattern known as the "Summer Triangle."

Sagittarius's stars make a pattern called the "Teapot," and its "spout" points at the bright, orangey star Antares.

Lyra & Hercules

Hercules is big, but its stars aren't very bright. Use Vega, in Lyra, to help you find it.

The Double Double

If you look at this star with a telescope, you'll see it split up into four different ones – two double stars close together.

Scientific name: Epsilon Lyrae
Visibility: dark skies
Look with: telescope
Difficulty to spot: ✶ ✶ ✶

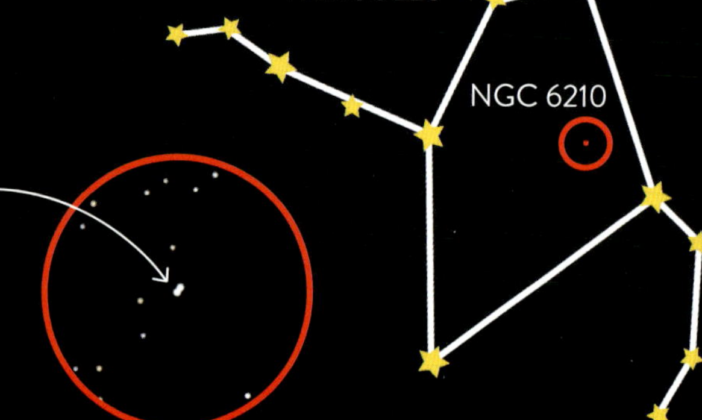

The Turtle Nebula

Four jets of very hot gas are firing out of the star that made this nebula. They look like the flippers of a turtle swimming through space.

Scientific name: NGC 6210
Visibility: very dark skies
Look with: telescope
Difficulty to spot: ✶ ✶ ✶ ✶ ✶

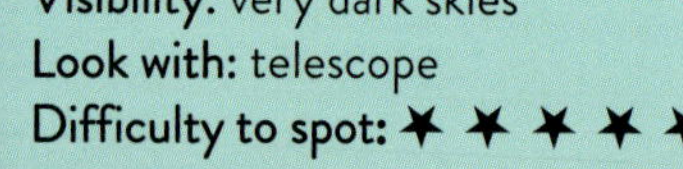

NGC 6791 Open Cluster

Can you see the yellow tint of this cluster's stars? That's because they're around eight billion years old (exceptionally ancient for an open cluster) and are slowly losing heat as they age.

Scientific name: NGC 6791
Visibility: dark skies
Look with: telescope
Difficulty to spot: ✶ ✶ ✶ ✶ ✶

Messier 92 Globular Cluster

One of the brightest globular clusters, and possibly the most ancient in our galaxy. Roughly 14 billion years old, it's almost the same age as the universe itself!

Scientific name: Messier 92 (M92)
Visibility: dark skies
Look with: telescope
Difficulty to spot: ✶ ✶ ✶

The Ring Nebula

The spectacular dying stages of a star, this amazing nebula looks like a heavenly smoke ring as the star at its center hurls off huge amounts of hot gas.

Scientific name: Messier 57 (M57)
Visibility: dark skies
Look with: telescope
Difficulty to spot: ✶ ✶ ✶

The Great Hercules Cluster

This is the northern sky's most magnificent globular cluster. In 1974, scientists beamed information about humans and life on Earth toward it, but the message will take 25,000 years to arrive.

Scientific name: Messier 13 (M13)
Visibility: dark skies
Look with: telescope
Difficulty to spot: ✶ ✶

Cygnus

Cygnus represents a swan in flight. Its brightest star, Deneb, is at the swan's tail.

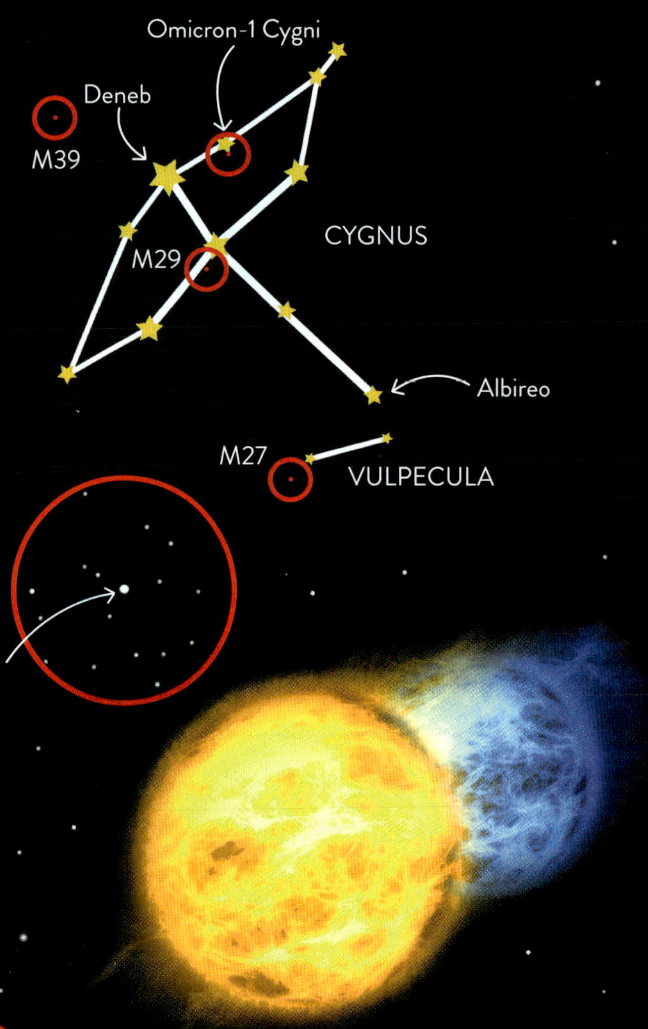

The cross-shaped pattern in Cygnus is called the "Northern Cross."

Albireo

Possibly the most beautiful double star in the night sky. Take a closer look to see two strikingly different stars – a brighter yellow one with a fainter blue companion.

Scientific name: Beta Cygni
Visibility: even in light-polluted skies
Look with: telescope
Difficulty to spot: ✶

The Cooling Tower Cluster

This cluster's uneven rectangle of stars looks a bit like a mini version of the Pleiades (p. 55). If dust in our galaxy didn't block its light, it would appear up to 1,000 times brighter!

Scientific name: Messier 29 (M29)
Visibility: even in light-polluted skies
Look with: telescope
Difficulty to spot: ✶ ✶ ✶

The Dumbbell Nebula

This huge bubble of gas around a dying star was the first of this type of nebula to be discovered, in 1764. It would look over 100 times brighter than the Sun if we were the same distance away.

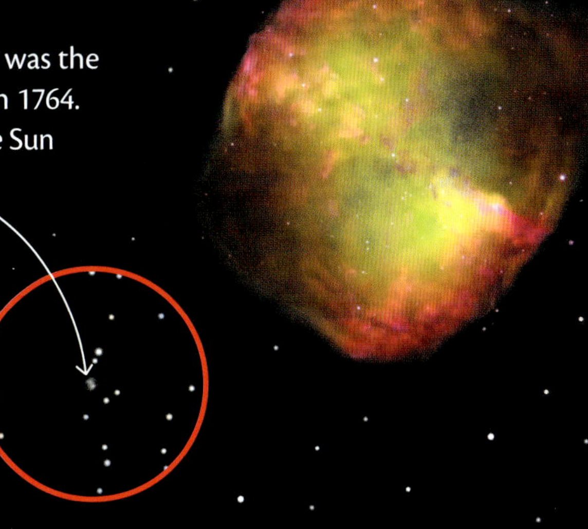

Scientific name: Messier 27 (M27)
Visibility: dark skies
Look with: telescope
Difficulty to spot: ✶ ✶ ✶

The Pyramid Cluster

At 200 to 300 million years old, this cluster's stars will soon swell and become "red giants." This makes it interesting for astronomers watching to learn more about what will happen to our Sun in a few billion years.

Scientific name: Messier 39 (M39)
Visibility: dark skies
Look with: telescope
Difficulty to spot: ✶ ✶ ✶

Triple Star

Three stars in Cygnus line up very closely with each other to create this beautiful triple star. Look for a burnt-orange star near to two others – one white, one blue.

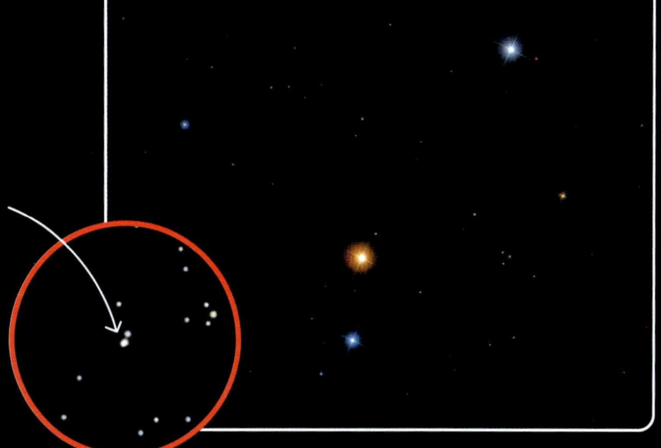

Scientific name: Omicron-1 Cygni
Visibility: even in light-polluted skies
Look with: telescope
Difficulty to spot: ✶ ✶ ✶ ✶

Aquila & nearby

Aquila represents an eagle. Altair, its brightest star, is one corner of the "Summer Triangle" pattern *(see page 27)*.

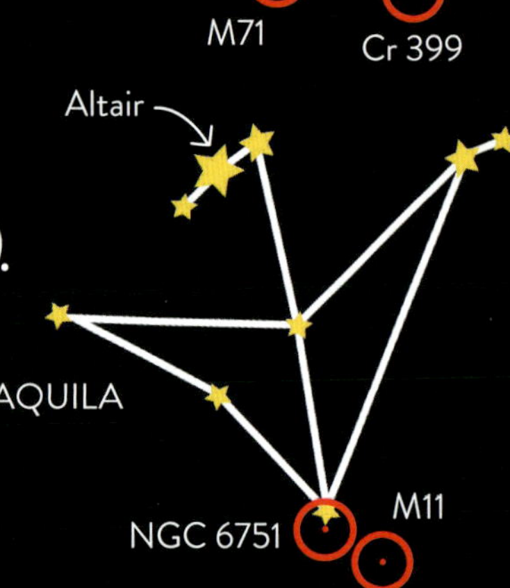

M14

Many of these sights are in other nearby constellations that are faint and much harder to find than Aquila.

M14 Globular Cluster

This cluster is all by itself, with nothing else to see nearby. It looks slightly oval-shaped, dim and distant in the empty black sky.

Scientific name: Messier 14 (M14)
Visibility: dark skies
Look with: telescope
Difficulty to spot: ✶ ✶ ✶

The Angelfish Cluster

"Only" nine or ten billion years old, this is one of the youngest and smallest globular clusters. It's not very round either, so people thought it was an open cluster for nearly 200 years.

Scientific name: Messier 71 (M71)
Visibility: dark skies
Look with: telescope
Difficulty to spot: ✶ ✶ ✶ ✶

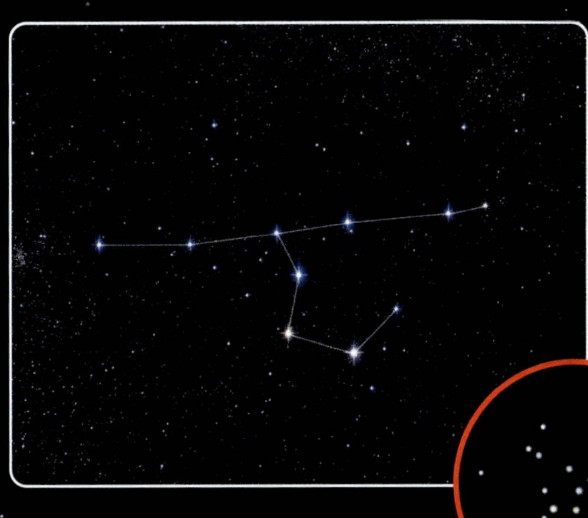

Brocchi's Cluster

Despite its name, this beautiful pattern of ten stars isn't actually a cluster. Can you see the line of stars and the hook shape near the middle? That's why it's also called the "Coathanger."

Scientific name: Collinder 399 (Cr 399)
Visibility: even in light-polluted skies
Look with: binoculars
Difficulty to spot: ✶

The Wild Duck Cluster

A stunning open cluster that's home to nearly 3,000 tightly packed stars. The brightest ones make a "V" shape, like a flock of ducks flying in formation.

Scientific name: Messier 11 (M11)
Visibility: dark skies
Look with: telescope
Difficulty to spot: ✶ ✶ ✶

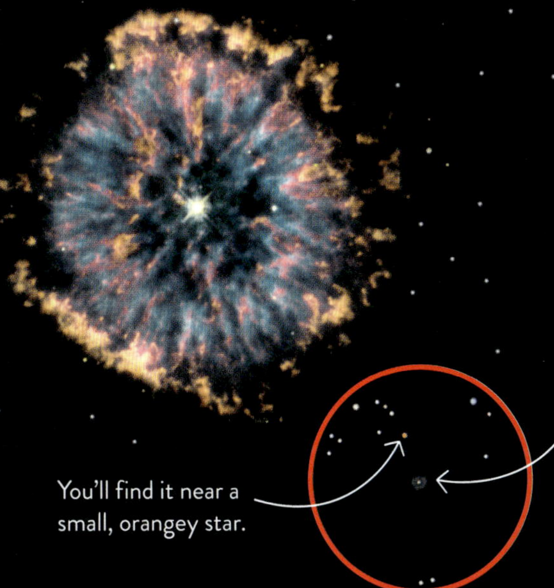

The Glowing Eye Nebula

Try looking for this object staring back at you from the depths of space. Created thousands of years ago from the gases of a dying star, it's about 600 times the size of our Solar System.

You'll find it near a small, orangey star.

Scientific name: NGC 6751
Visibility: very dark skies
Look with: telescope
Difficulty to spot: ✶ ✶ ✶ ✶ ✶

Ophiuchus & Serpens

These two linked constellations cover a large area of sky that doesn't have many stars.

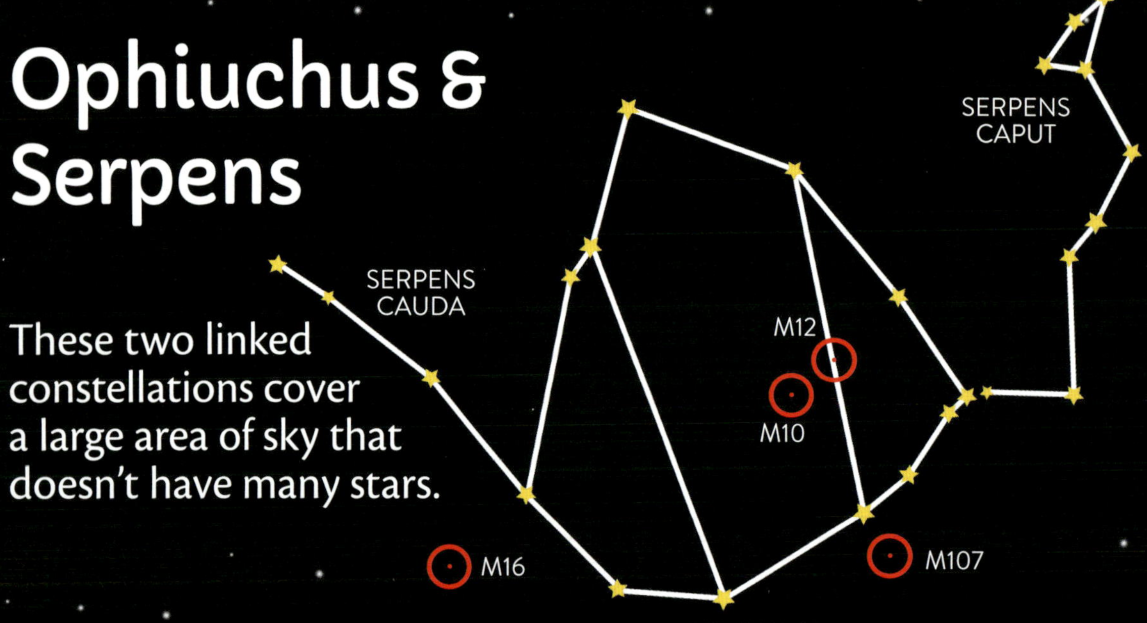

The Flickering Globular

Huge forces near the middle of our galaxy are pulling this ball of stars out of shape. It was the first globular cluster in the Milky Way to have a black hole found inside it.

Scientific name: Messier 62 (M62)
Visibility: dark skies
Look with: telescope
Difficulty to spot: ✶ ✶ ✶ ✶

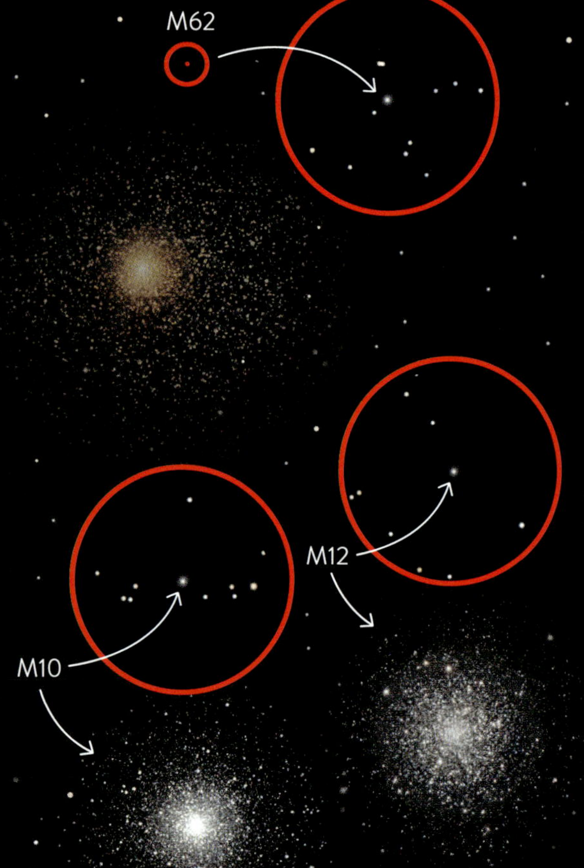

The Gumball Globular

You can spot this globular cluster very close to another one – Messier 10. Its many bright stars look like straggly feelers. What shapes can you imagine in the dark gaps between them?

Scientific name: Messier 12 (M12)
Visibility: dark skies
Look with: telescope
Difficulty to spot: ✶ ✶ ✶

The Crucifix Cluster

One of the most ancient globular clusters, nearly 14 billion years old. Its stars are fairly spread out, so you can see them like bright faces in a crowd.

Scientific name: Messier 107 (M107)
Visibility: dark skies
Look with: telescope
Difficulty to spot: ✶ ✶ ✶ ✶

The Rose Cluster

Most of the stars in this globular cluster are almost three times the age of our Solar System. The younger blue ones inside it were "born" when some of the older stars crashed into each other.

Scientific name: Messier 5 (M5)
Visibility: dark skies
Look with: telescope
Difficulty to spot: ✶ ✶ ✶ ✶

The Eagle Nebula

This bright gas cloud looks a bit like an eagle that's soaring through space. It's famous for the "Pillars of Creation" – vast columns of gas that have been discovered inside it.

Scientific name: Messier 16 (M16)
Visibility: dark skies
Look with: binoculars or telescope
Difficulty to spot: ✶ ✶ ✶

Messier 16 is also known as the "Star Queen Nebula."

Sagittarius

The sky around Sagittarius is teeming with stars because it lies in front of the bright heart of our galaxy.

The middle of the Milky Way looks like a puff of steam above the "spout" of Sagittarius's "Teapot" shape.

The Omega Nebula

Also known as the "Horseshoe Nebula," the "Swan Nebula," and the "Lobster Nebula," this incredible sight is full of newly-born stars, and is one of the biggest and brightest nebulas in our galaxy.

Scientific name: Messier 17 (M17)
Visibility: dark skies
Look with: binoculars or telescope
Difficulty to spot: ✶ ✶ ✶

The Great Sagittarius Cluster

This was one of the first globular clusters ever discovered, in 1665, and is among the brightest and closest ones to us. Scientists think that it may contain as many as 100 black holes.

Scientific name: Messier 22 (M22)
Visibility: dark skies
Look with: telescope
Difficulty to spot: ✶ ✶ ✶

Messier 28 Globular Cluster

This cluster is home to about 50,000 stars. The small, collapsed core of one of them has been found spinning incredibly fast – over 300 times a second!

Scientific name: Messier 28 (M28)
Visibility: dark skies
Look with: naked eye
Difficulty to spot: ✶ ✶ ✶

The Lagoon Nebula

Intensely bright new stars are being born in this giant gas cloud. It's named after the darker, lagoon-like shape near its core, which almost splits the nebula in two.

Scientific name: Messier 8 (M8)
Visibility: dark skies
Look with: binoculars or telescope
Difficulty to spot: ✶ ✶ ✶

Lagoon-shaped lane

The Trifid Nebula

This unusual sight is three different nebulas in one. The dark "cracks" in the pink and blue ones are the dense, dusty veins of a third nebula that runs through them.

Scientific name: Messier 20 (M20)
Visibility: dark skies
Look with: telescope
Difficulty to spot: ✶ ✶ ✶

Scorpius

Scorpius, the scorpion, lies quite close to the horizon in the summer sky.

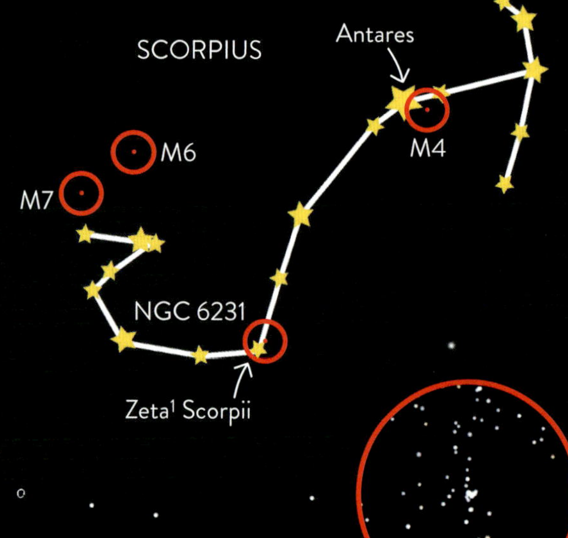

Try to go to a dark, open space to spot these sights low down in the sky.

The Baby Scorpion Cluster

Also called the "Northern Jewel Box," this cluster has over a hundred stars that gleam like diamonds. One of them, Zeta[1] Scorpii, is an incredible 850,000 times brighter than the Sun!

Scientific name: NGC 6231
Visibility: dark skies
Look with: telescope
Difficulty to spot: ✶ ✶ ✶

An image of the Butterfly Cluster with lines to show its insect-like shape.

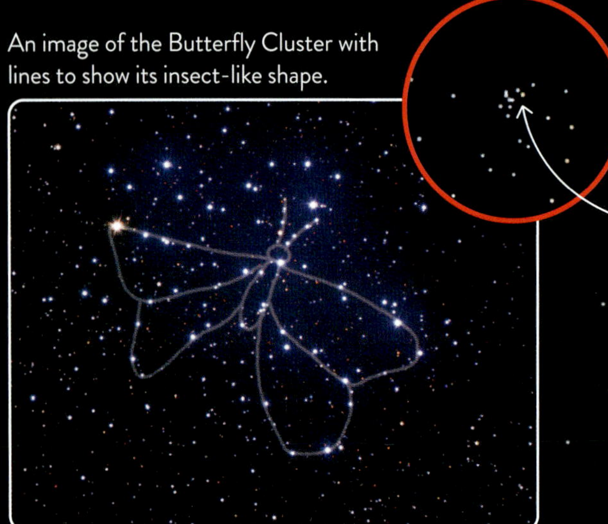

The Butterfly Cluster

Look for this cluster near the "sting" of Scorpius's tail and you'll see a few dozen glittering stars. Can you imagine the shape of a butterfly in the pattern they make?

Scientific name: Messier 6 (M6)
Visibility: dark skies
Look with: binoculars or telescope
Difficulty to spot: ✶ ✶ ✶

The Ptolemy Cluster

Your eyes can easily make out this pretty open cluster, which has been known about since ancient times. It's named after the astronomer who first recorded seeing it, way back in 130 CE.

Scientific name: Messier 7 (M7)
Visibility: even in light-polluted skies
Look with: naked eye or binoculars
Difficulty to spot: ✶ ✶ ✶

Antares

This "red supergiant" star is nicknamed "the heart of the Scorpion," and it really does pulse! One of the biggest stars your eyes can see, and if it swapped places with our Sun, it would swallow up Mercury, Venus, Earth and Mars!

The above photo of Antares, from 2017, is the most detailed ever taken of a star other than the Sun.

Scientific name: Alpha Scorpii
Visibility: even in light-polluted skies
Look with: naked eye
Difficulty to spot: ✶

The Spider Cluster

The closest globular cluster to us. One of its stars has a planet orbiting it that's over twice as massive as Jupiter and nearly three times as old as our Solar System.

Scientific name: Messier 4 (M4)
Visibility: dark skies
Look with: telescope
Difficulty to spot: ✶ ✶ ✶

Fall star maps

To use these star maps, face either north or south during the fall. Then, compare the map for that direction to the stars you can see in the sky.

LOOKING NORTH

The constellations which are best seen in the fall are shown in orange.

Western horizon

Eastern horizon

LOOKING SOUTH

Eastern horizon

Western horizon

These maps are approximate guides for where to look – your view of the stars changes depending on where you are and the time of night.

Fall star patterns

Look for a large "W"-shaped pattern of stars high in the north sky. That's called Cassiopeia, and you can use it to find other fall star patterns.

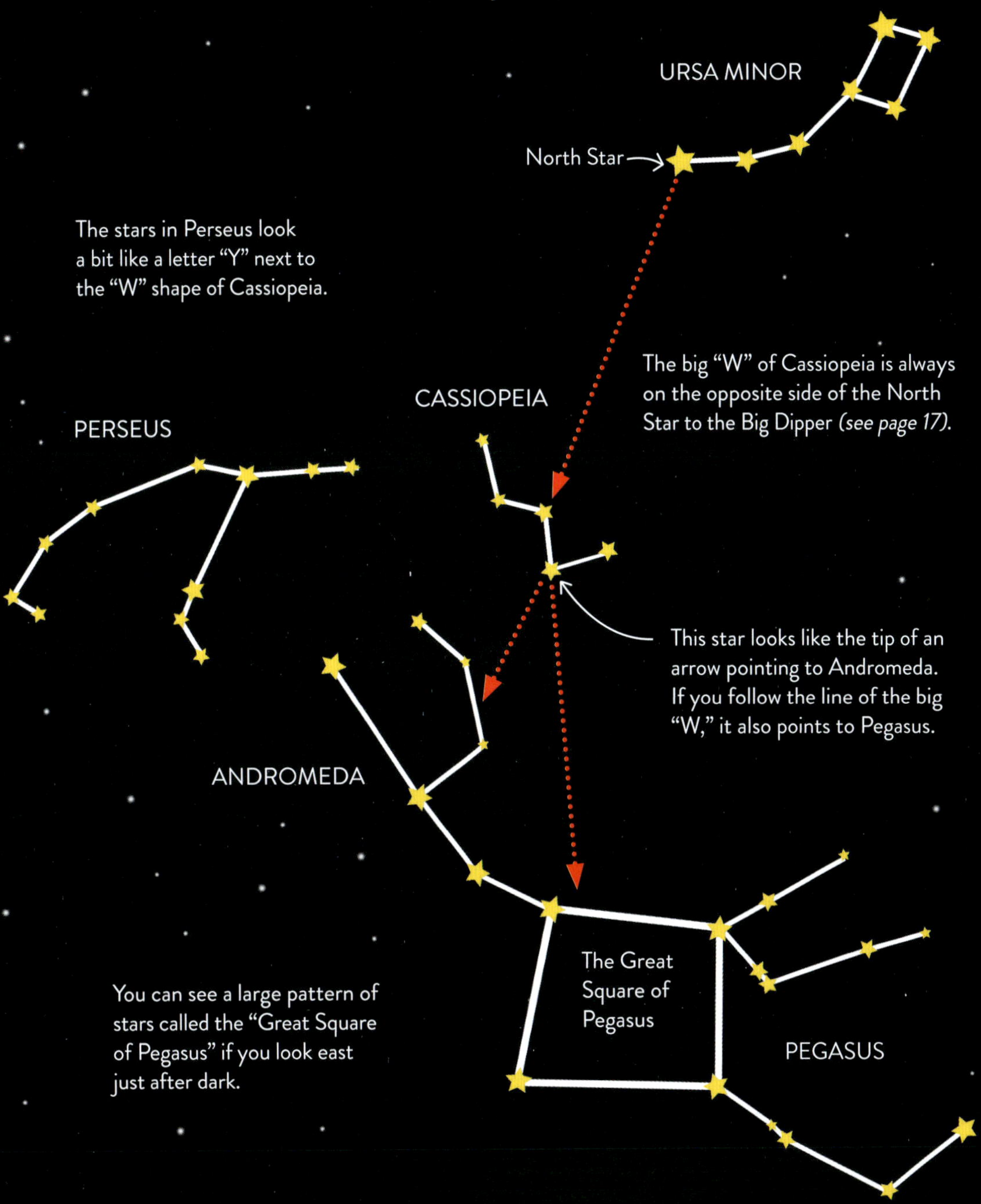

Cassiopeia & Perseus

In many places, you can see Cassiopeia's "W" shape and the "Y" of Perseus all year round.

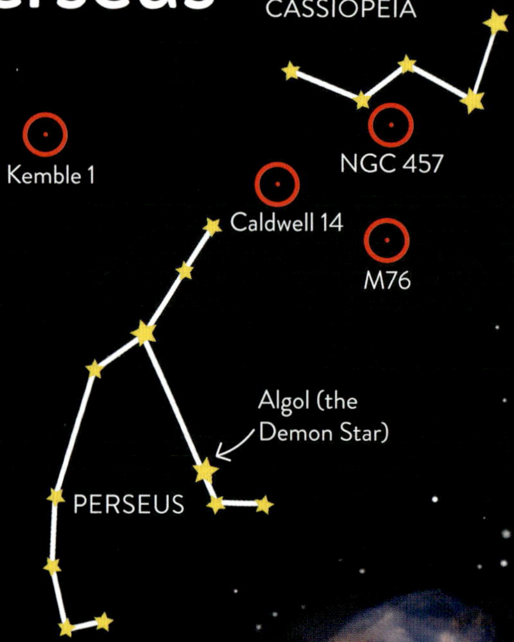

CASSIOPEIA

NGC 457

Kemble 1

Caldwell 14

M76

Algol is a variable star. You can watch as it brightens and dims over three days – it's three times brighter at its brightest than at its faintest.

Algol (the Demon Star)

PERSEUS

The Little Dumbbell Nebula

This cloud of gas around a dying star looks like a balloon that's been pinched in the middle. It might look similar to the Ring Nebula (p. 29) if we could see it at the same angle.

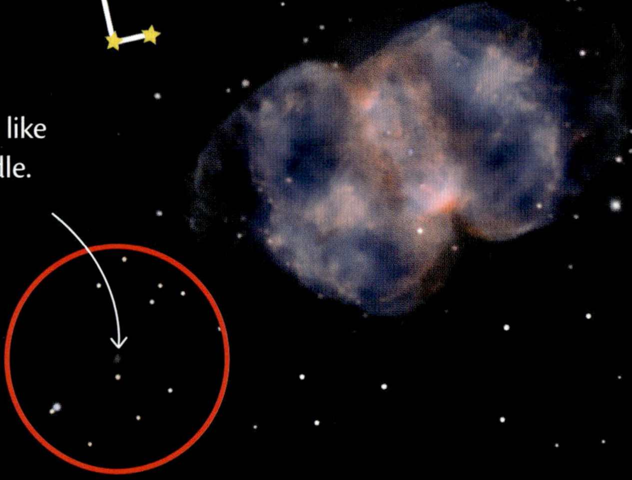

Scientific name: Messier 76 (M76)
Visibility: very dark skies
Look with: telescope
Difficulty to spot: ✶ ✶ ✶ ✶ ✶

The Double Cluster

These two overlapping open clusters make a wonderful sight to look at with binoculars – hundreds of sparkling blue-white stars, scattered across the sky.

Scientific name: Caldwell 14
Visibility: dark skies
Look with: binoculars or telescope
Difficulty to spot: ✶ ✶ ✶

The Perseids

These fast-flying shooting stars leave long, colorful trails, and they create spectacular displays in the summer sky between midnight and dawn.

Scientific name: The Perseids
Visibility: dark skies
Look with: naked eye
Difficulty to spot: ✶

There can be 60 or more shooting stars an hour at the Perseids' peak, which is around August 12th–13th.

Kemble's Cascade

During early evenings in the fall, look for this enchanting pattern that tumbles down like a waterfall toward an open cluster's "pool" of stars.

Scientific name: Kemble 1
Visibility: dark skies
Look with: binoculars or telescope
Difficulty to spot: ✶ ✶

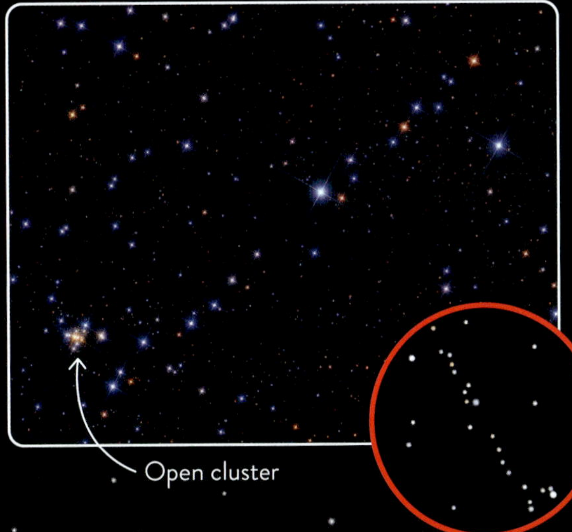

Open cluster

The Dragonfly Cluster

Also known as the "Owl Cluster," or the "E.T. Cluster" after the alien in a famous movie. Imagine its stars as two bright eyes, and a fainter body with its wings (or arms) outstretched.

Scientific name: NGC 457
Visibility: dark skies
Look with: telescope
Difficulty to spot: ✶ ✶ ✶

The two bright "eyes"

Andromeda & Pegasus

Look for the star pattern called the "Great Square of Pegasus" to find these two linked constellations.

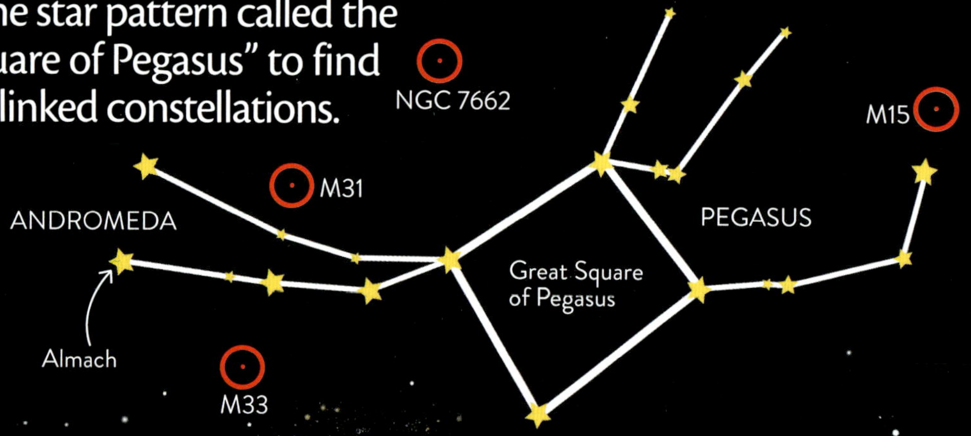

NGC 7662

M15

M31

ANDROMEDA

PEGASUS

Great Square of Pegasus

Almach

M33

The Andromeda Galaxy

The light you see from this galaxy left it 2.5 million years ago, when humans barely existed! It's on course to collide with our own galaxy in a few billion years' time.

Scientific name: Messier 31 (M31)
Visibility: dark skies
Look with: telescope
Difficulty to spot: ✶ ✶ ✶

The Andromeda Galaxy is the closest large galaxy to ours, and contains more than twice as many stars.

Almach

If you look at this beautiful double star through a telescope, it will split into two remarkably different stars – one bright and golden, one dimmer and indigo-blue.

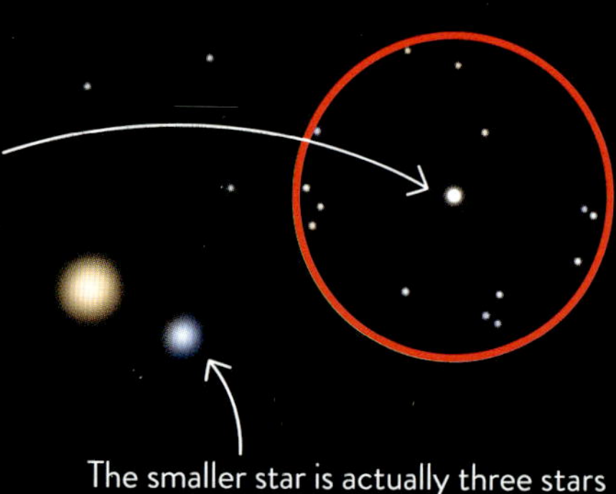

The smaller star is actually three stars orbiting each other, so Almach is made up of four stars in total.

Scientific name: Gamma Andromedae
Visibility: even in light-polluted skies
Look with: naked eye; telescope to split
Difficulty to spot: ✶

The Triangulum Galaxy

This is the second-closest large galaxy to ours, but it's tricky to spot. The light from its billions of stars is very spread out, so it's a large but dim patch in our sky.

Scientific name: Messier 33 (M33)
Visibility: very dark skies
Look with: telescope
Difficulty to spot: ✶ ✶ ✶ ✶ ✶

The Blue Snowball Nebula

The gases of a dying star created this wintry-looking nebula about 3,000 years ago. Can you spot it, like a small, bluish disc that's dimmer at the edges?

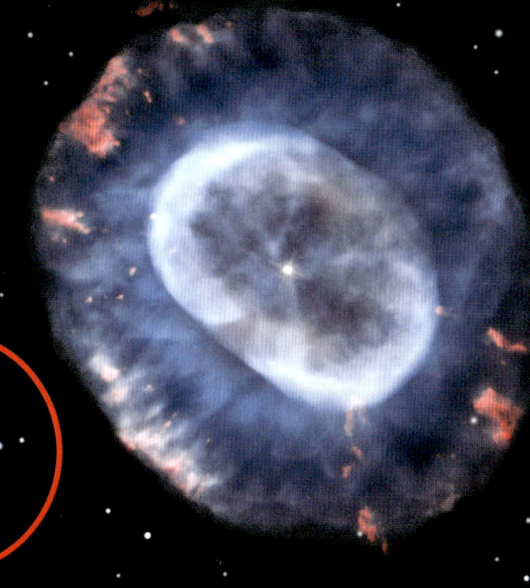

Scientific name: NGC 7662
Visibility: dark skies
Look with: telescope
Difficulty to spot: ✶ ✶ ✶

The Great Pegasus Cluster

This magnificent, ancient ball of stars is one of our galaxy's densest globular clusters. There are over 100,000 stars inside, all circling a massive black hole at its center.

Scientific name: Messier 15 (M15)
Visibility: dark skies
Look with: telescope
Difficulty to spot: ✶ ✶

Aquarius & Capricornus

Aquarius is very faint, so try to find the "Y" shape of its "head" near to Capricornus.

Aquarius represents a water-carrier, while Capricornus is a sea goat – a mythical creature that's half fish, half goat.

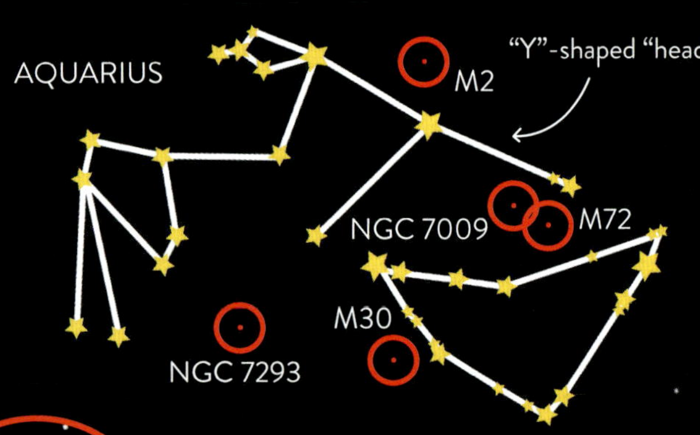

Messier 72 Globular Cluster

A very distant ball of stars that's relatively small and spread out. It looks a bit like a city that you see out of a plane's window at night.

Scientific name: Messier 72 (M72)
Visibility: dark skies
Look with: telescope
Difficulty to spot: ✶ ✶ ✶ ✶

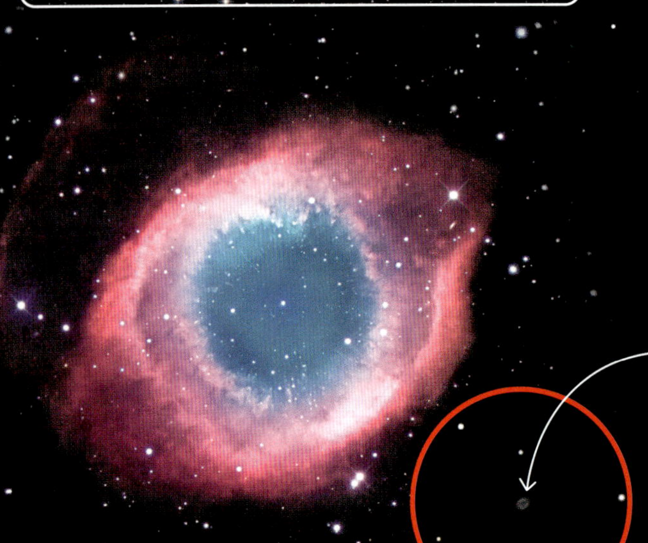

The Helix Nebula

Roughly 10,500 years old, this glowing cloud of gas around an ageing star is nicknamed the "Eye of Sauron" – the fiery eye of the Dark Lord in *The Lord of the Rings*.

Scientific name: NGC 7293
Visibility: dark skies
Look with: telescope
Difficulty to spot: ✶ ✶ ✶ ✶

Messier 30 Globular Cluster

This very dense cluster moves in the opposite direction to most things in the Milky Way, so scientists think that it was ripped away from a smaller galaxy in the distant past.

Scientific name: Messier 30 (M30)
Visibility: dark skies
Look with: telescope
Difficulty to spot: ✶ ✶ ✶

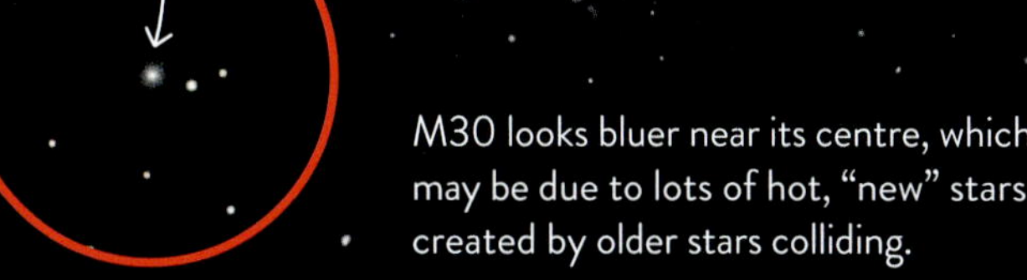

M30 looks bluer near its centre, which may be due to lots of hot, "new" stars created by older stars colliding.

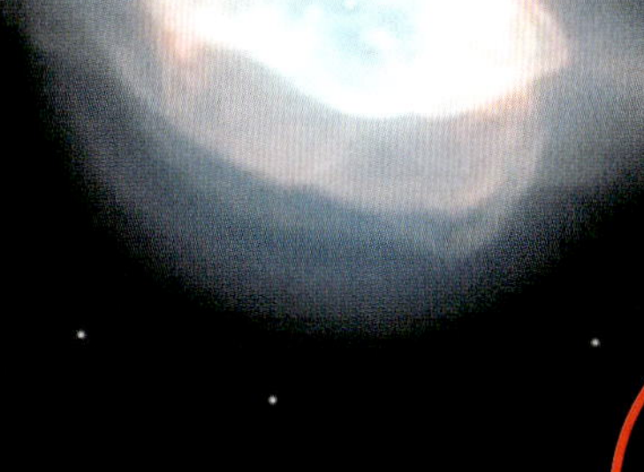

The Saturn Nebula

Can you see how this nebula looks like a blurred view of the famous ringed planet Saturn in our own Solar System?

Radiation from the dying star at the center of the Saturn Nebula gives it a greenish glow.

Scientific name: NGC 7009
Visibility: dark skies
Look with: telescope
Difficulty to spot: ✶ ✶ ✶ ✶

Messier 2 Globular Cluster

At around 12.5 billion years old and home to about 150,000 stars, this is one of our galaxy's oldest and largest globular clusters.

Scientific name: Messier 2 (M2)
Visibility: dark skies
Look with: telescope
Difficulty to spot: ✶ ✶ ✶

Winter star maps

To use these star maps, face either north or south during the winter. Then, compare the map for that direction to the stars you can see in the sky.

LOOKING NORTH

The constellations which are best seen in the winter are shown in blue.

Western horizon

Eastern horizon

LOOKING SOUTH

Eastern horizon

Western horizon

These maps are approximate guides for where to look – your view of the stars changes depending on where you are and the time of night.

Winter star patterns

If you look east at nightfall, you'll see a line of three bright stars. They form "Orion's Belt," and you can use them to find lots of other patterns in the winter sky.

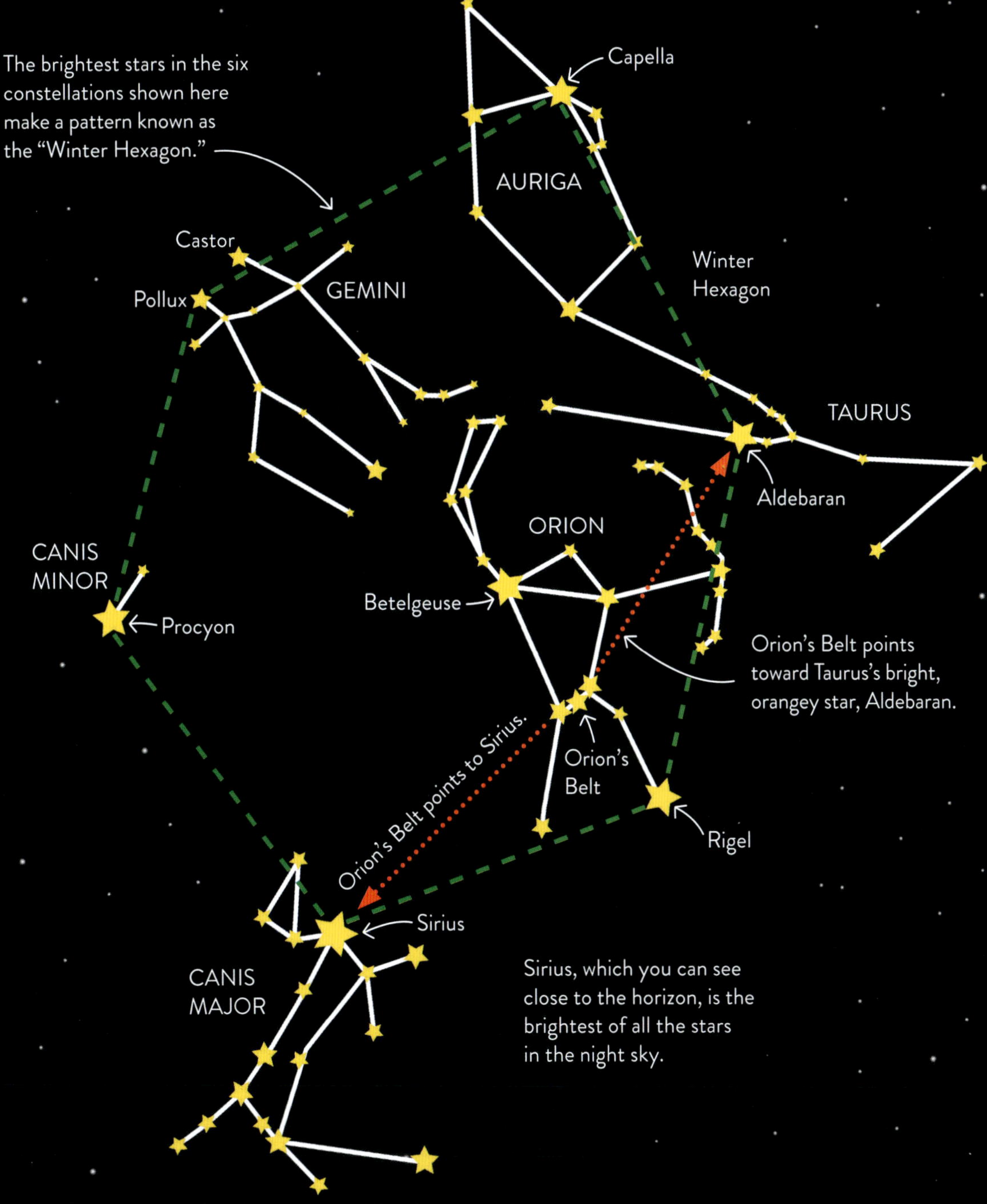

Orion & Lepus

Orion the hunter dominates the winter sky. Look for the line of three bright stars in his belt.

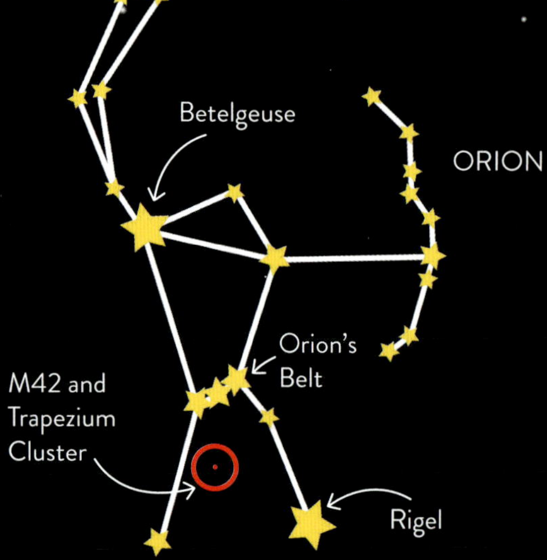

Lepus represents a hare that Orion is chasing.

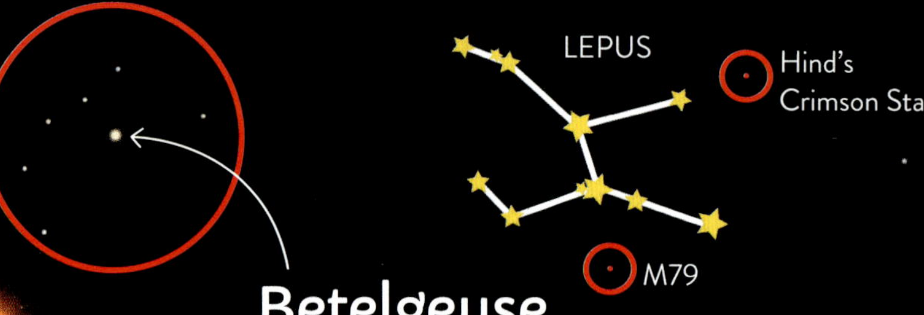

Betelgeuse is pronounced "Bet-ell-gurze," but some people say "Beetle Juice."

Betelgeuse

This enormous orange star at Orion's shoulder throbs like a heart, slowly swelling and shrinking. Very rarely, when it's at its biggest, it outshines Rigel and becomes Orion's brightest star.

Scientific name: Alpha Orionis
Visibility: even in light-polluted skies
Look with: naked eye
Difficulty to spot: ✶

Hind's Crimson Star

Here's another star whose brightness changes. Named after the astronomer who discovered it, this star looks most "crimson" when it's at its dimmest, around every 14.5 months.

Scientific name: R Leporis
Visibility: dark skies
Look with: telescope
Difficulty to spot: ✶ ✶ ✶ ✶ ✶

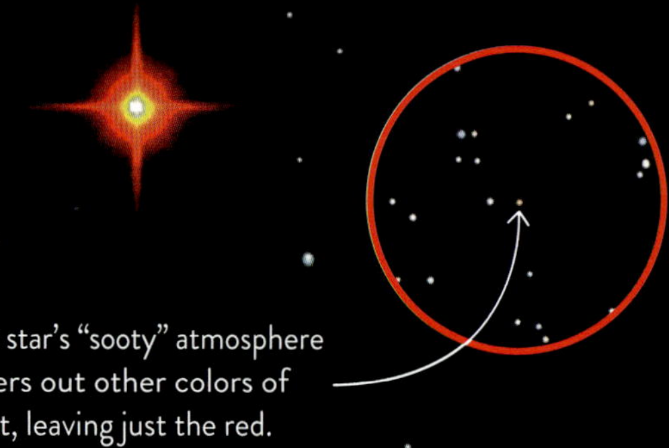

The star's "sooty" atmosphere filters out other colors of light, leaving just the red.

The Trapezium Cluster

Look for this little cluster glowing at the heart of the Orion Nebula. It's named for the shape of its four bright stars, one of which is over 250,000 times brighter than our Sun.

Scientific name: Theta-1 Orionis
Visibility: even in light-polluted skies
Look with: telescope
Difficulty to spot: ✶ ✶

Trapezium Cluster

The Orion Nebula

Lots of new stars are being born inside this beautiful nebula – the brightest one in our sky. It's the fuzzy second "star" down in a faint line called "Orion's Sword."

Scientific name: Messier 42 (M42)
Visibility: even in light-polluted skies
Look with: binoculars or telescope
Difficulty to spot: ✶ ✶

Lepus Globular Cluster

One of the winter sky's brightest, this is in a different part of our galaxy to most globular clusters. Astronomers think the Milky Way pulled it in from a smaller galaxy long ago.

Scientific name: Messier 79 (M79)
Visibility: dark skies
Look with: telescope
Difficulty to spot: ✶ ✶ ✶ ✶

Canis Major & Monoceros

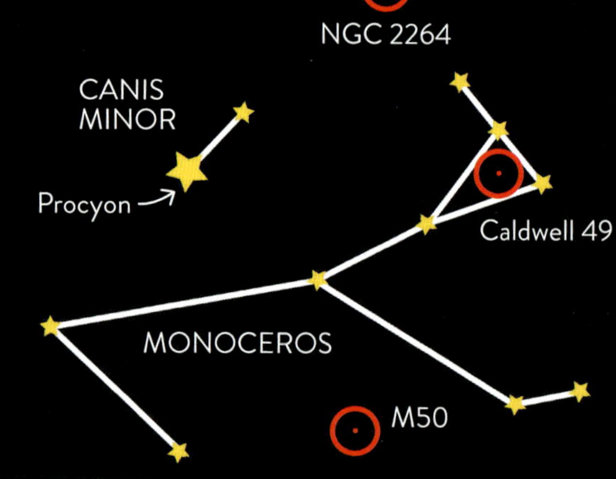

Monoceros's faint stars represent a unicorn between Canis Major and Canis Minor – the "Great Dog" and the "Little Dog."

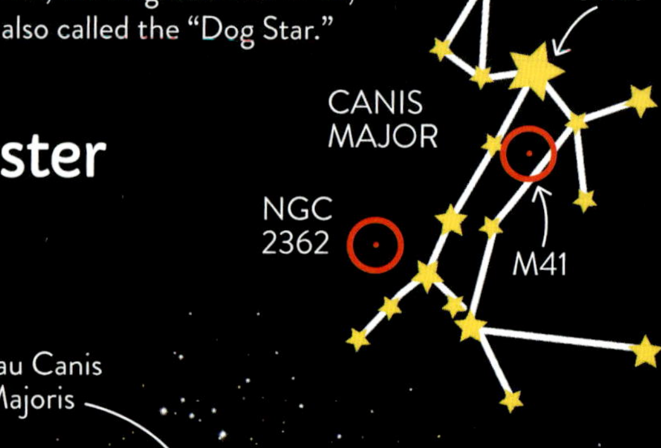

The Tau Canis Majoris Cluster

Look for this beautiful cluster close to the horizon. The very bright star that it's named after shines like a brilliant white diamond among its dimmer companions.

Scientific name: NGC 2362
Visibility: dark skies
Look with: telescope
Difficulty to spot: ✶ ✶ ✶

The Heart-Shaped Cluster

Can you spot the shape of a heart in this cluster? Most of its stars shine faintly blue, but look for a sprinkling of yellowish ones around its edges, and a large orangey one below its center.

Scientific name: Messier 50 (M50)
Visibility: dark skies
Look with: telescope
Difficulty to spot: ✶ ✶ ✶ ✶

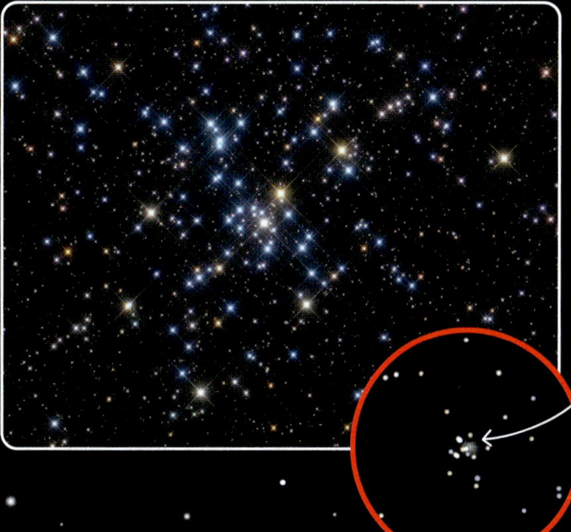

The Little Beehive Cluster

The Greek philosopher Aristotle might have seen this cluster as early as 325 BCE, when he wrote about "a dim star with a tail." It makes a lovely sight, twinkling just below Sirius.

Scientific name: Messier 41 (M41)
Visibility: dark skies
Look with: binoculars or telescope
Difficulty to spot: ✶ ✶

The Rosette Nebula

About 2,500 young stars have been born inside this vast gas cloud. A hole has been blown in the middle of it by the cluster of blue stars you can see – the brightest two are firing out 400,000 times more energy than the Sun!

Scientific name: Caldwell 49
Visibility: dark skies
Look with: telescope
Difficulty to spot: ✶ ✶ ✶ ✶ ✶

The Christmas Tree Cluster

This open cluster's stars look like ornaments decorating a toppled-over Christmas tree. The shape of the tree is formed by the surrounding clouds of the Cone Nebula.

Scientific name: NGC 2264
Visibility: dark skies
Look with: telescope
Difficulty to spot: ✶ ✶ ✶

Taurus

Taurus represents the horned head and front half of a bull, and is full of magnificent sights.

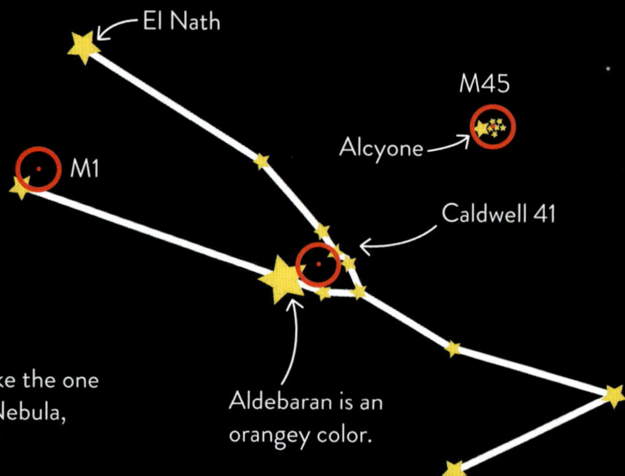

Huge star explosions, like the one that created the Crab Nebula, are called "supernovas."

The Crab Nebula

The magnificent remains of a gigantic star that exploded in 1054. It was called a "guest star" by astronomers at the time because the supernova was bright enough to be seen in full daylight.

Scientific name: Messier 1 (M1)
Visibility: very dark skies
Look with: telescope
Difficulty to spot: ✶ ✶ ✶ ✶ ✶

The Hyades

This is the closest star cluster to Earth, and an amazing sight with binoculars. Its brightest stars make a "V" shape with the orangey star Aldebaran.

Scientific name: Caldwell 41
Visibility: even in light-polluted skies
Look with: naked eye or binoculars
Difficulty to spot: ✶

Halloween Fireballs

Around Halloween, you can see five to ten of these shooting stars an hour. Some are spook-tacular "fireballs" that are as bright as the Moon, and leave smoky trails.

Scientific name: The Taurids
Visibility: dark skies
Look with: naked eye
Difficulty to spot: ✶

Around midnight is the best time to see the Taurids.

The Pleiades

A stunning cluster that's also known as the "Seven Sisters" – but you'll probably only see six stars with your eyes, shimmering like sapphires. With binoculars, it looks just like a mini version of the Big Dipper (p. 18).

Scientific name: Messier 45 (M45)
Visibility: even in light-polluted skies
Look with: naked eye or binoculars
Difficulty to spot: ✶

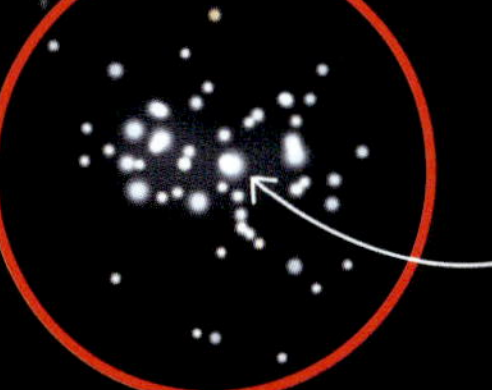

Alcyone

This blue-white star is the brightest in the Pleiades. 2,000 times brighter than the Sun, and ten times wider, it bulges at its center because it's spinning at 149km (96 miles) a second!

Scientific name: Eta Tauri
Visibility: even in light-polluted skies
Look with: binoculars or telescope
Difficulty to spot: ✶

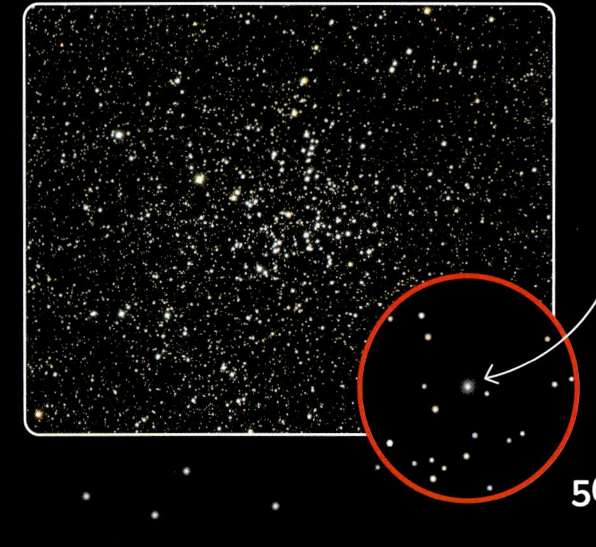

The Starfish Cluster

The brighter stars near the middle of this cluster make a shape like a starfish, or a crooked cross. One of these giant stars is 900 times brighter than our Sun.

Scientific name: Messier 38 (M38)
Visibility: dark skies
Look with: telescope
Difficulty to spot: ✶ ✶ ✶ ✶

The Aurigids

These shooting stars are created by dust from a comet that only orbits the Sun once every 2,500 years. Very rarely, bursts of up to 200 an hour trace long blue and green trails in the sky.

Scientific name: The Aurigids
Visibility: dark skies
Look with: naked eye
Difficulty to spot: ✶ ✶

The Pinwheel Cluster

This cluster is similar in size to the Pleiades (p. 55), and would be just as bright and spectacular if it wasn't ten times further away. Look for a dozen or so stars in a shape like an "X."

Scientific name: Messier 36 (M36)
Visibility: dark skies
Look with: telescope
Difficulty to spot: ✶ ✶ ✶ ✶

The Salt and Pepper Cluster

At around 350 to 550 million years old, this is very ancient for an open cluster. It's the biggest and brightest of the three in Auriga, sprinkled with over 500 stars.

Scientific name: Messier 37 (M37)
Visibility: dark skies
Look with: telescope
Difficulty to spot: ✶ ✶ ✶ ✶

Gemini

Gemini represents a pair of twin brothers from Greek mythology whose names were Castor and Pollux.

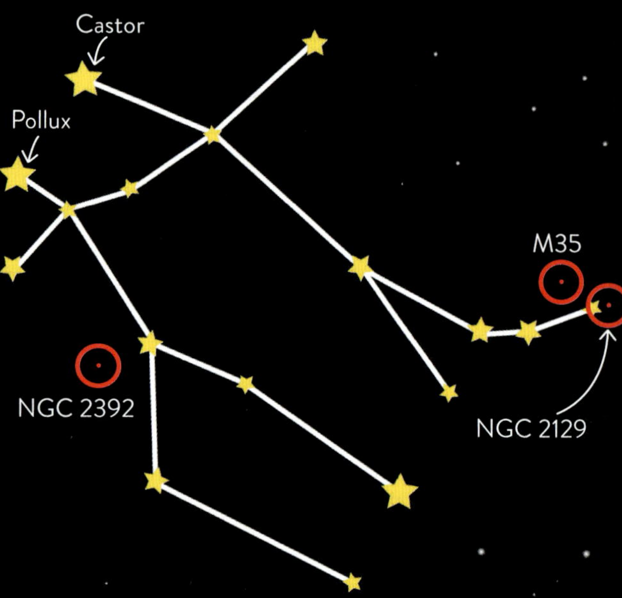

Gemini's two brightest stars are also called Castor and Pollux. They represent the twins' heads.

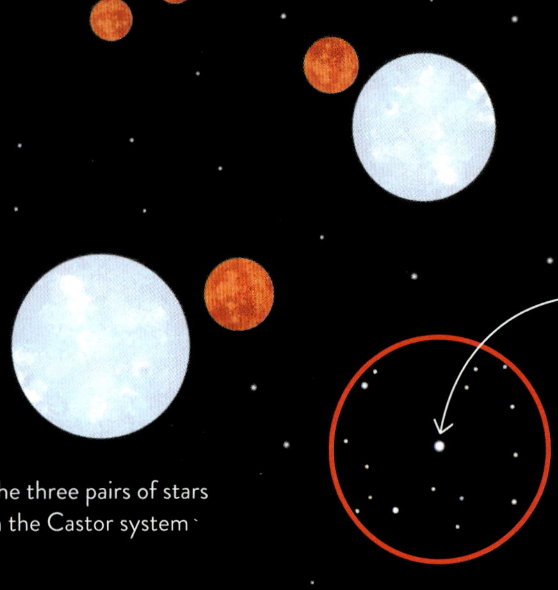

The three pairs of stars in the Castor system

Castor Star System

The second-brightest point in Gemini, Castor is actually six stars. Made up of three pairs, you'll see two stars with a telescope, and possibly a third very small, faint one.

Scientific name: Alpha Geminorum
Visibility: even in light-polluted skies
Look with: naked eye; telescope to split
Difficulty to spot: ✶ ✶

The Geminids

Hundreds of slow-moving shooting stars fly all across the sky in these spectacular winter showers. Unusually, they come from an asteroid, not a comet *(see page 61)*.

Scientific name: The Geminids
Visibility: dark skies
Look with: naked eye
Difficulty to spot: ✶

The Shoe-Buckle Cluster

Named for its shape, this bright cluster of about 400 stars can be found, fittingly, near to Castor's "foot." It's one of the best open clusters to spot.

Scientific name: Messier 35 (M35)
Visibility: dark skies
Look with: binoculars or telescope
Difficulty to spot: ✶ ✶ ✶

The Lion Nebula

A beautiful nebula that looks like a lion's golden mane around red, open jaws. It began forming about 10,000 years ago from the thrown-off gases of the dying star at its center.

Scientific name: NGC 2392
Visibility: very dark skies
Look with: telescope
Difficulty to spot: ✶ ✶ ✶ ✶

NGC 2129 Open Cluster

This very young, distant cluster is dominated by two bright stars close together. The other dimmer ones swarm around the pair, like fireflies darting around bright lights.

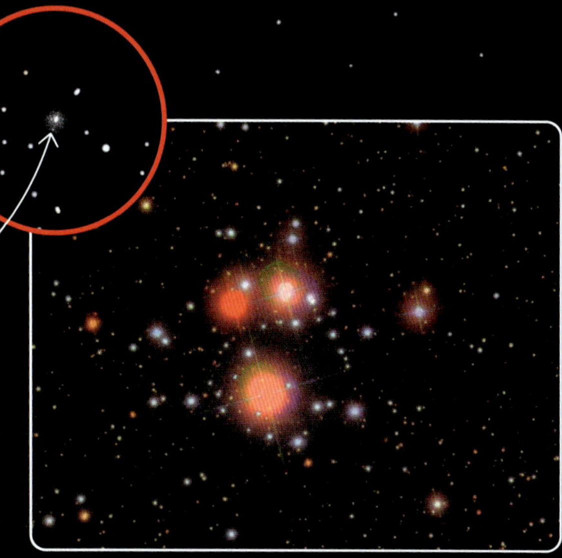

Scientific name: NGC 2129
Visibility: dark skies
Look with: telescope
Difficulty to spot: ✶ ✶ ✶ ✶ ✶

More sights to see

Here are some other things you can look for in the night sky.

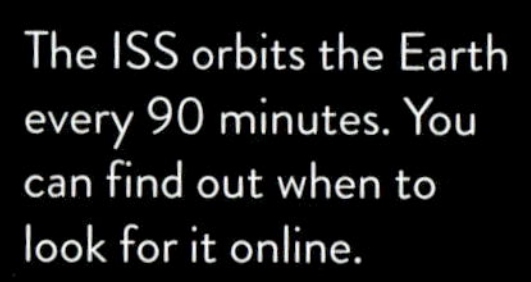

The ISS orbits the Earth every 90 minutes. You can find out when to look for it online.

Satellites

The space around our planet is full of artificial satellites, such as the International Space Station (ISS). Watch for them crossing the sky like wandering stars.

Noctilucent Clouds

Try to spot the beautiful bands, streaks and waves of these "night shining clouds" during summer, at late dusk or early dawn.

The Milky Way

If you look south on clear, moonless nights, you can gaze into the heart of our own galaxy! It looks like a misty, milky cloud of millions of stars spilled across the sky.

You'll get some of the best views of the Milky Way around September.

Asteroids

Millions of these rocky, metallic or icy objects orbit the Sun. A few of them are sometimes bright enough to see with binoculars as tiny dots of light.

Go online to see where and when to look for asteroids at their brightest.

Meteor showers

Showers of shooting stars whiz across the night sky at certain times of year. They're made as the Earth moves through rivers of dust left behind by comets, and the dust enters our atmosphere in fiery streaks.

There's a list of the best times to see different meteor showers on page 63.

Comets

Look for the blue-white, dusty tails of these giant "dirty snowballs." They stream across our night sky for a few short weeks as they hurtle close to the Sun.

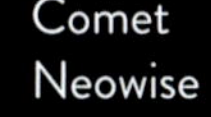

Comet Neowise

About one comet every couple of years is bright enough to be seen with the naked eye.

The Northern Lights

Glowing curtains and beams of green, red and purple light fill the sky in these otherworldly displays. Usually you can only see them in the far north, but sometimes they're visible from further south, too.

The Northern Lights are caused by radiation from the Sun hitting the Earth's atmosphere.

Star types

There are all sorts of stars, shining blue, white and orange in our night sky. Here are some of the ones you'll see.

Red supergiant

Red supergiant

The largest type of star. The biggest ones are called "hypergiants" and could fit billions of stars the size of our Sun inside them. They look more yellowy-orange than red.

Blue supergiant

These huge, hot, bright stars burn through their fuel quickly, and only "live" for millions of years, not billions.

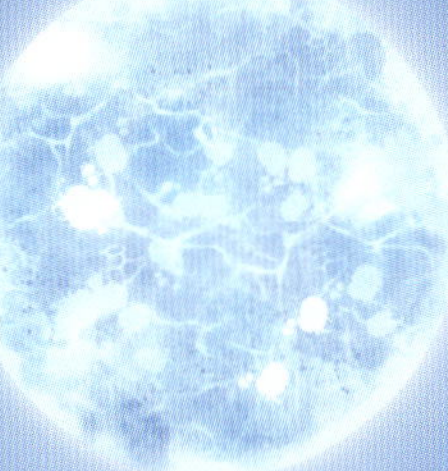

Blue supergiant

Blue giant

These large, hot stars are much rarer than red giants. Some blue giants shine millions of times more brightly than our Sun.

Blue giant

Red giant

An old star that has run out of fuel, and grown much bigger. Our Sun will become one in a few billion years.

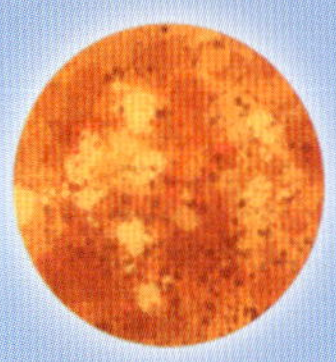

Red giant

Carbon star

Usually a red giant with a "sooty" atmosphere that makes it look redder than most others.

Carbon star

Yellow dwarf

A star like our Sun. Most of them look white in the night sky, not yellow.

Yellow dwarf

Red dwarf

The most common type of star, but none is big and bright enough to see from Earth with the naked eye.

Red dwarf

White dwarf

The dying Earth-sized remains of a star like our Sun.

White dwarf

The brightest stars in the northern night sky

Some of these stars only look so bright because they're much closer to us than others.

No.	Star name	Constellation	Type of star	Best seen	Page no.
1	Sirius	Canis Major	Bluish mid-life star	Winter	52
2	Arcturus	Boötes	Red giant	Spring	20
3	Vega	Lyra	Bluish mid-life star	Summer	28
4	Capella	Auriga	A pair of yellow giants	Winter	56
5	Rigel	Orion	Blue supergiant	Winter	50
6	Procyon	Canis Minor	Yellowish mid-life star	Winter	52
7	Betelgeuse	Orion	Red supergiant	Winter	50
8	Altair	Aquila	White mid-life star	Summer	32
9	Aldebaran	Taurus	Red giant	Winter	54
10	Antares	Scorpius	Red supergiant	Summer	39
11	Spica	Virgo	Blue giant	Spring	24
12	Pollux	Gemini	Red giant	Winter	58

Meteor showers to look for

You may have to stay up late or get up very early to see some of these shooting stars.

Name of shower	Where to look	When to look	Peak activity
Quadrantids	Boötes	December 28th to January 12th	January 4th
Lyrids	Lyra	April 14th to 30th	April 22nd
Perseids	Perseus	July 17th to August 24th	August 12th
Orionids	Orion	October 2nd to November 7th	October 21st
Leonids	Leo	November 6th to 30th	November 17th
Geminids	Gemini	December 4th to 20th	December 14th

Index

Picture Credits

© Science Photo Library: p.3 (tr) Detlev van Ravensway; p.3 (b) Mark Garlick; p.6 (mr), p.18 (br) Davide De Martin; p.7 (ml), p.23 (br), p.29 (bl), p.32 (ml), p.46 (bl), p.53 (bl) Robert Gendler; p.9 (br) Miguel Claro; p.14 (ml) John Sanford; p.22 (ml) David Ducros; p.22 (br) John Chumack; p.31 (br), p.43 (ml), p.44 (bm), p.52 (mr) Gerard Lodriguss; p.32 (br), p.47 (tr), p.52 (bl) NOAO / AURA / NSF; p.39 (ml) European Southern Observatory; 50 (br) Damian Peach; p.51 (bl) NASA, ESA, STSCI, F. Ferraro (Universita Di Bologna) and S. Djorgovski (Caltech); p.58 (bl) Jeff Dai; p.61 (ml) Walter Pacholka, Astropics

© Alamy Stock Photo: Front Cover (b) Mark Garlick / Science Photo Library; p.6 (ml) Pandorum BS; p.12 (ml) Cristian Cestaro; p.14 (mr), p.21(ml) Alan Dyer/VWPics; p.14 (br) Hemis; p.15 (tm) Galaxy Picture Library; p.20 (br), p.21 (br), p.23 (tr), p.23 (ml), p.33 (tl), p.33 (mr), p.35 (br), p.37 (bl), p.43 (br), p.45 (tl), p.53 (mr), p.54 (br), p.59 (tr), p.61 (bm) Stocktrek Images Inc; p.24 (bl), p.25 (mr), 47 (br) NASA Image Collection; p.30 (mr) Skorzewiak; p.30 (bl), p.31 (ml), p.34 (bm), p.37 (mr), p.38 (bl), p.39 (br), p.56 (bl) Science History Images; p.34 (br) Westend61 GmbH; p.36 (mr) Irina Dmitrienko; p.42 (bl) Pere Sanz; p.43 (tr) Orest Shvadchak; p.50 (ml) Łukasz Szczepanski; p.51 (tl) Granger – Historical Picture Archive; p.51 (mr) Giulio Ercolani; p.55 (ml) Nature Picture Library; p.56 (mr) Franco Tognarini; p.60 (tr) Geopix; p.60 (ml) Algirdas Sinkevicius; p.60 (bl) Daniel Holmes; p.61 (tr) Paul Fleet; p.61 (bl) All Canada Photos

© NASA: Front Cover (m), Back Cover (m), p.1 (b), p.6 (tr), p.7 (tr), p.7 (mr), p.9 (tr), p.10 (br), p.11 (tr), p.11 (br), p.12 (tr), p.12 (br), p.12&13 (b), p.13 (tr), p.13 (ml), p.13 (br), p.14 (tr), p.15 (tl), p.19 (br), p.20 (ml), p.21 (tr), p.24 (mr), p.25 (bl), p.28 (ml), p.28 (bl), p.29 (tl), p.29 (mr), p.31 (tr), p.33 (bl), p.42 (mr), p.44 (ml), p.45 (mr), p.45 (bl), p.54 (ml), p.57 (tr), p.57 (mr), p.59 (ml), p.59 (br) NASA; p.7 (bl) GALEX, JPL-Caltech, NASA; p.8 (r) NASA / Bill Dunford; p.10 (m), p.11 (ml) NASA / GSFC / Arizona State University; p.14 (ml), p.15 (bl), p.15 (bm) NASA / JPL; p.14 (br) NASA / JPL-Caltech / USGS; p.15 (mr) NASA / ESA / STScl / A. Simon / R. Roth; p.18 (ml) X-ray: NASA / CXC / SAO, Optical: Detlef Hartmann, Infrared: NASA / JPL-Caltech; p.19 (mr), p.25 (tl) NASA, ESA & the Hubble Heritage Team (STScl/AURA); p.25 (tl) Event Horizon Telescope Collaboration; p.35 (tr), p.35 (ml) ESA / Hubble & NASA; p.37 (tl) ESA / Hubble & NASA. J.E.Grindlay et al.; p.46 (ml) NASA, ESA, Hubble, HPOW; p.47 (ml) NASA, ESA

© Shutterstock: p.4 (br) 1981 Rustic Studio kan; p.6 (bl) Raymond Cassel; p.9 (ml) italnazca; p.19 (tl) Whitelion61; p.34 (m) PlanilAstro; p.36 (bl) David Hajnal; p.38 (mr), p.53 (tl), p.57 (bl) Tragoolchitr Jittasaiyapan; p.39 (tr) Brian Donovan; p.55 (tr) AstroStar; p.55 (br) Nazarii_Neshcherenskyi

© Celestron: p.5 (tr); p.5 (bm)

First published in 2025 by Usborne Publishing Limited, 83–85 Saffron Hill, London ECIN 8RT, United Kingdom. usborne.com
 AE. First published in America 2025.